# FAITHFUL PARENTS
# FAITHFUL CHILDREN

## Why We Homeschool

Donald W. Schanzenbach

Publisher:
River City Press, Inc.
4301 Minneapolis, MN 55412
t 888.234.3559
www.rivercitypress.net
publisher@rivercitypress.net

Cover Design and layout by Erika Schanzenbach, Bristol, Tennessee

First Edition Printed in the United States of America

ISBN 0-9776713-4-8

Mission to Restore America
Bristol, Tennessee
www.missiontorestoreamerica.com
don@missiontorestoreamerica.com
1-866-390-1570 toll free

Don Schanzenbach is also the author of *Advancing the Kingdom*. *Advancing the Kingdom* is a worldview study focusing on sixteen areas of culture including: history, literature, mathematics, philosophy, the arts, and more. It will guide you through Scripture to a Biblical understanding of these topics. For ordering information please go to our website, www.missiontorestoreamerica.com.

# PREFACE

This book is designed for you to give to friends who ask, "Why do you homeschool?" It lays out the Biblical case for homeschooling, leaving no wiggle room for Christians who sincerely accept God's Word as authoritative. It will also prove to be an encouragement to those who have already begun to obey God in how they educate their children.

California State Senator Teresa Hughes states. "We live in a society where children going to school have become comparable to soldiers going off to war."[1] *Faithful Parents Faithful Children* will demonstrate some of the evidence for this perspective and show parents Biblical reasoning to combat the assumptions behind the present systems.

An abundance of words have been typed about the educational opportunities and disasters awaiting our children. However, after reviewing the available books discussing home education I decided there was a need for a foundational study that would present the Biblical basis for education. There are other works describing the horrendous condition of the government schools but they typically do not demonstrate much about what the Scriptures teach. My primary goal in writing this book was to work out Biblical doctrine related to education and to present that doctrine in a single, easily readable manuscript. The book is designed for broad general reading but retains the careful logic and interpretation found in conservative theological treatises.

Also, I was unable to discover any book defending homeschooling that covered the highly important connections between home education, generational thinking and covenantal living. I believe that the church needs to recover its thinking and practices to reflect what God has told us concerning these things. It is impossible to plan for successive Christian generations while sending our children to school. The schools undermine all of the most important work of the family, especially as relates to education.

Having homeschooled all three of our children through their high school years we want to share some of what we have learned along the way. The homeschool movement has advanced greatly since we began in the early 1980s. Yet there are ever more young parents just beginning to venture into this practice. For each family it is an experience that engenders both fear of failure and eager anticipation as to how God will bless the quavering step of obedience; and He will bless it. God desires good for His people and He is the rewarder of those who seek Him.

# ACKNOWLEDGEMENTS

Thank you to all who have assisted in the work on this book. Karin Balgaard, Daniel and Rachel Schanzenbach, Charlie Chase, Dan Williamson, and both of my daughters—your suggestions and corrections were invaluable. Special thanks to Rev. Laurence Windham our beloved pastor who took time to read the manuscript and give several useful suggestions. Double thanks to my wife Christine who encourages me in everything.

# Contents

# CHAPTER 1

# God Commands Parents to Educate

And he said unto them, Set your hearts unto All the
words which I testify among you this day, which ye
shall command your children to observe to do, all
the words of this law.

**Deuteronomy 32:46**

God, in His word, has clearly commanded parents to teach their
children. It is to the church that God has given His written Word.
From the beginning His people have been blessed with immutable
truth. This greatest of books is rightly understood as God's revelation
concerning all things necessary for life. The prophet Jeremiah wor-
shipped saying, "Thy words were found, and I did eat them; and thy
word was unto me the joy and rejoicing of mine heart: for I am called
by thy name, O Lord God of hosts" (Jeremiah 15:16).

To eat God's word, to be filled, feasting, chewing, and digest-
ing the meat is our blessed calling, even as it was for Jeremiah. The
Biblically minded man rejoices. His heart is leaping, dancing in joy
at the arrival of his Father's food. Nothing could surpass it. Why?
Because he is called by the name of the Lord God of hosts. He is
Christian. Christ lives in him, the Master with the servant. With

every savory bite the honor of being called by His name is delivered fresh to his mind. His love for his Lord overwhelms his senses and he pledges his very life in memory of the Earnest (Eph. 1:14) first given him.

What have we said? How have we lived? Do our actions demonstrate a heart wholly devoted to the Lord whose name we carry? When we pronounce in our faith statements that God's word is our sole rule for faith and practice do we believe this, or are they just words, pious gush? Walk with me through some Scriptures and we will pick from the word a few selections and lift them out for closer inspection. What has God commanded concerning education?

## MOSES ON EDUCATION

One of the key Scriptures delineating God's mind is found in Deuteronomy 6:6–9:

> And these words, which I command thee this day, shall be in thine heart: And thou shalt teach them diligently unto thy children, and shalt talk of them when thou sittest in thine house, and when thou walkest by the way, and when thou liest down, and when thou risest up. And thou shalt bind them for a sign upon thy hand, and they shall be as frontlets between thine eyes. And thou shalt write them upon the posts of thy house, and on thine gates.

There are thirty-four chapters in the book of Deuteronomy. The first five act as an introduction to the book. The sixth gives instructions and warnings concerning its use. Chapters seven through twenty-seven reveal the heart of God's law, making up the core. After this come the promised blessings and cursings, for obedience or disobedience, for God's people, in chapters twenty-eight and twenty-nine. The balance of the chapters serve to give additional warnings and to close out the Pentateuch.

This giving of the law carries high importance in God's order. The law is given twice; once in Leviticus and again, with additional details, in Deuteronomy. The law is not only the heart of the Pentateuch and Deuteronomy but provides the foundation for all of Biblical culture in both testaments. Consequently the New Testament writers refer to it often to build doctrine, settle disputes, and explain the mind of God.

## THE IMPORTANCE OF DILIGENCE

This unassailable position of the law, sets for us a framework for understanding the importance of the command mentioned above. It is the parents that are to do this work. Parents are responsible to teach these truths "when thou sittest in thine house, and when thou walkest by the way, and when thou liest down, and when thou risest up" which pretty much means all the time it would seem. God made it impossible for His people to misunderstand His will. There is nothing obtuse here. The Creator's intention is that the children are to be on a continuing program of learning from their parents during their waking hours. This is not taken care of by spending a few minutes in after dinner devotions or sending the children off to a Sunday school class for one hour a week. The spirit of the passage communicates this is an all day, every day, way of life. It is not to be done in a haphazard or lazy manner. This teaching work is to be performed diligently morning through evening.

Why the concern for diligence? Why are such specific commands given that encompass the daily routine? The entire concept of teaching as a way of life is foreign to us. It speaks of a different age and a lost culture that revolved around the family and the home. We often hear that we cannot turn back the clock, meaning that to wed family, traditions, work, and daily routine is impossible now. It is an era to which we cannot return. Yet the command of God stands

" …when thou walkest by the way…when thou liest down…when thou risest up…"

## CULTURE AND EDUCATION

We have been told that this command is cultural. My reply is, "Of course it is cultural." The very purpose of God's commands is to show His people how to build God-pleasing culture. A highly important part of Christian culture is the rearing and training of Christian seed. This can only be accomplished under obedience to God's commands for the family. In this case, concerning the education of the children, we are told to be about this business of education as a full time affair. We are instructed to be diligent because the sin nature of mankind is trying to prevail in every child. The natural man (child) does not seek God nor know Him. Careful instruction is required.

When we first started educating our children at home we thought of it as school at home. Thus we tried to imitate the teaching style found in the schools. We slowly discovered that the entire teaching enterprise needs to be understood in light of Biblical ideals. We do not need to imitate either the style or the exact content taught in the schools. Teaching may be done in ways that are more integral to good family life. The schedule and rhythm of the family along with the work and duties of the family have to be maintained. Education is a part of all of this. It is done in concert with family life not in opposition to it. Teaching children becomes a natural part of what the family does. It is a part of Christian culture.

The notion that culture should be separated from the disciplines or corrections of Scripture is ludicrous. Where do we find any Biblical teaching that culture may be formed outside of the Biblical model? Technologies improve, and this is a good thing. But the underlying norms of behavior, family duties, morals, church duties, etc. are always to be patterned after God's revealed will. We are not allowed to discount Biblical example or instruction due to the present culture being at odds with them. In fact the real need in our time is to recover Biblical culture, not to continue to live in opposition to it. Do we esteem Biblically-based culture so lightly that we sincerely believe the present immoral and disobedient culture is superior?

My wife and I spent the early years of our marriage in membership at a local Bible church with an attendance of around one hundred seventy-five. We were the first couple in the church to educate our children at home. A second and third family soon joined us in that behavior. Now the years have passed. Our children and theirs, twelve between the three families, are mostly grown and are all solid Christians. Out of the entire balance of that church we are able to identify less than ten other children that serve Christ today. Almost all of the children from that church are either marginal Christians or outright humanists/pagans. Yet all the way along our home education journey we ran up against excuses, resistance, and being told we would harm our progeny if we did not rear them like other parents were doing. The idea of resisting the culture was unthinkable to most of the families around us.

Christians that are unwilling to challenge the culture in this area of education often lose their kids. The humble believer in God's word and works can rear Godly children best by extricating his family from the present educational systems. The ways of the God of the Bible are sufficient for our day. Biblical culture is good and right because it is rooted in good and right precepts from the Creator Himself. For us to discount Biblical culture is to discount the God of that culture. It is a supremely arrogant attitude and deeply mistaken.

# DILIGENCE

As Christians we are in a sense at a disadvantage to the world. The unregenerate masses may act according to their nature. By acting and teaching in a manner natural to their desires, and to the culture, they produce children after their own kind; children that are utterly lost. They naturally resist God at every point. It begins at birth and is as ordinary as breathing. But the Christian religion requires its adherents to actively teach all of the attributes of Biblical civilization. It is an education that must address every aspect of thinking and living. It has to bring truth to all things and instruct the heart and will of the child in every thing. The Christian life is not communicated to the next generation merely by telling a few stories or holding a doctrine class. It is brought to them in daily life. We are to be making Scriptural observations and instruction as we "walk by the way" with them. Doctrine must be taught formally in the home, but it is also caught while hearing stories and receiving instruction at the table and the bedside. Christian teaching must be a life style not an event. Diligence is paramount if any success is to be expected.

As we advanced in our home education enterprise we became aware of many opportunities to teach our children important lessons about life as they appeared around us. I spent all of my parenting years working as a self-employed carpenter. I often took my children with me as I looked at projects, presented bids, and performed the work. Consequently, I was able to explain to them the correct manners and Christian attitudes to display under various circumstances. If a bid was rejected I could try to teach them a Biblical attitude toward rejection and loss. If a project went well I could discuss with them attitudes of thankfulness or humility toward God. None of this could be possible if the children had never met the customers or seen the projects. Having walked, by the way with me, they were able to see our beliefs worked out in real life. There is no stronger teaching environment.

This importance of diligent teaching is strengthened near the end of Deuteronomy in chapter thirty-two verses forty-six and forty-seven. The text reads:

> And he said unto them, Set your hearts unto all the words which I testify among you this day, which ye shall command your children to observe to do, all the words of this law. For it is not a vain thing for you; because **it is your life**: and

through this thing ye shall prolong your days in the land...
[Emphasis mine].

It was no mean thing for Moses to instruct that obedience to the details of God's law was their life. This diligent pursuit of His will was what guaranteed His covenant people a prolonged stay in the land. Every word, each idea must be as familiar as the lines on their hands or the silhouette of the hills in the evening light. To have only a passing familiarity with His commands would not suffice. God's word was to be their life. The oracles of God were not to be in their lives, they were to be life itself. All of life was to have a holy direction. The people were to be consumed in their passion for Godly righteousness. Anything less dishonors the God who spoke from a burning bush. The entire landscape of our lives is to be holy ground.

## The Heart Condition

Moses urges the people "set your hearts unto all the words I testify among you..." What would it mean to set our hearts unto all these words? Is the condition of our hearts such that we will dedicate all of our lives to the study and application of them? Setting the heart is much more intense, more given to the task than just studying or memorizing or knowing. Knowledge of God's words is just the beginning. Setting the heart includes meditation, commitment, daily pursuit in obedience, and a continuing application. My wife and I are members of a church where the people so value God's word that they are ever in discussion about its meaning and application. In church, at home, in gatherings during the week, they have made the Scriptures, and God's will, the center of what they discuss and do. There is no wall between real life and Christian behavior. It is all one. This is what it means to set the heart on the words of God.

When we are told that we cannot turn back the clock there is an assumption that changes in society are inexorable and final. This idea is demonstrably false. After all, if the status of society cannot be changed, why are we not still living in that more primitive state? The fact is that change toward a better model is quite possible. A return to a more family based life style is both possible and desirable if we are to gain a foothold against the avalanche of humanism rumbling across the landscape. In this regard we *must* turn the clock back if we want to make any progress at all. To those who say it is impossible, we say with Moses, "it is not a vain thing" to obey God and it will prolong our days in the land. It is God's promise. We may begin with our own families. More than a few have done so.

## RELEVANCE OF THE OLD TESTAMENT

Having begun this chapter using the law of Moses I am certain to receive complaints saying, "but that is Old Testament, those commands were intended for Israel not for the church." Be patient, we will arrive at the New Testament text soon enough, and it will confirm what the book of Deuteronomy teaches. However, let's remember what Paul told Timothy in his second letter saying "All Scripture is given by inspiration of God, and is profitable for doctrine, for reproof, for correction, for instruction in righteousness: that the man of God may be perfect, thoroughly furnished unto all good works" (2 Timothy 3:16–17). When Paul wrote this admonition it necessarily referred to the Old Testament since the New was still in the process of being written. It had not been finalized.

It is significant to note that the first use for which the church was to apply the Old Testament scripture was doctrine. Without realizing it many evangelicals have discounted the Old Testament as a source for doctrine. We use its stories for moral instruction and we find the history interesting, but we would never use Old Testament Scripture to build doctrine. It is thought that doctrine should only be derived from the New Testament. Yet Paul's first use was for doctrine. Verse seventeen in Second Timothy three shows the expected benefit of applying that doctrine "That the man of God may be perfect, furnished unto every good work."

The application is straightforward. By building good doctrine from the above cited passages in Deuteronomy the modern man of God will advance toward perfection of his walk and be "furnished unto every good work." In this case the good work is the proper instruction of his children. It is the preparation of his seed to live righteously in the land. He will establish his family as a bulwark against the rising generation of humanistically oriented radicals. Nothing could be more needed in the church and society than such righteous offspring. God has given us the method for educating them. We are to speak of God's words "when thou walkest by the way, and when thou liest down, and when thou risest up..." This is God's will for us.

Some Christians will argue that commands in Deuteronomy are only applicable for religious instruction, and are not intended to cover *regular* school subjects such as history, math, geography, biology etc. These parents see a sharp division between the supposed secular and sacred avenues of inquiry. This false dichotomy erects a barrier between the things about which God is concerned and those He supposedly is not. There is an assumption that good morals and prayer are all God cares about, and that He has little concern for more worldly pursuits or education. Yet if we look into the book of Deuteronomy itself we find God addressing law (almost the entire book), foreign policy (Deut. 7:20–24), economics (Deut. 8:13–18), land ownership (Deut. 10:14), sociological concerns (Deut. 14:28–29), warfare (Deut. 20), and other academic subjects, each as an integral part of His word. All of the created order is the Lord's. All of it is designed to be sacred. There is nothing rightly categorized as secular. God rules over the totality of His creation. Therefore all things must be taught from a Godly perspective if we are to please Him. There are no secular subjects. The book of Deuteronomy and the Scriptures in general may not be confined to a circle of knowledge separate from so-called school subjects.

# UNITY OF KNOWLEDGE

If we go now to Psalm eighty-six we can see how the appeal of David reflects the need for a unity in all we teach. David wrote this Psalm while under persecution from his enemies. He writes in verse fourteen "O God, the proud are risen against me, and the assemblies of violent men have sought after my soul; and have not set thee before them." We are not given details as to what the exact conflict was but we can read that "the proud are risen" against him, those who "have not set thee before them." We also live in such a time. The proud proposers of the religion of Humanism mock our faith in their classrooms daily. They teach every subject as if God is irrelevant or in many instances rail against His teaching. They will not allow our God to be set before them. Thus when we send our children to be educated in a non-Christian environment we bring disunity to our children's minds and hearts. The cause would not have been exactly the same, but it is this type of disunity that David prays against in verse eleven. He writes, "teach me thy way, O Lord; I will walk in thy truth: unite my heart to fear thy name."

It is this unity of heart that we seek for our children. Notice that David links teaching, walking in the truth, and uniting his heart in a single statement. These concepts are indissolubly linked. We are to teach all things from a Biblical perspective. This will give motivation to walk in the truth (understand life Biblically and obey God in all things), and will unite our children's minds around Godly thoughts. This is part of the cure for the double-minded man against which the New Testament preaches. The Old Testament doctrine cures the New Testament disease. Biblically based teaching has this purpose. It is the duty of parents to impart the unity of knowledge and faith to their children.

Solomon understood these principles of teaching and the unity of knowledge. He addresses his book of Proverbs to his son saying "My son, hear the instruction of thy father, and forsake not the law of thy mother: for they shall be an ornament of grace unto thy head, and chains about thy neck" (Proverbs 1:8–9). This great king believed that teaching was to be given by the father and the mother. The duty was no one's but theirs. A man who by all accounts could have assigned the work to hirelings of some kind, deigned to do the work himself, thus his saying, "my son, hear the instruction of thy father." The teaching was to include two major parts: instruction which was more general and the law which was very specific. Every Jewish boy had to understand the law of God. The law gave the basis for understanding the mind of God. At the beginning of Proverbs, chapter four, Solomon gives more detail saying, "Hear, ye children, the instruction of a father, and attend to know understanding. For I give you good doctrine, forsake ye not my law." Thus the father and the mother placed God's law at the heart of the teaching. It was their duty to impart these critical words to their son. Solomon understood these ideas about education but failed to live an obedient life as an example for his children. We are not likely to be wiser than Solomon but we can be more obedient, thus giving our children both teaching and example by which to pattern their lives.

## THE BEAUTY OF WISDOM

Proverbs chapter one, verse nine, tells us that the teaching of the parents will be "an ornament of grace unto thy head, and chains about thy neck." Our teaching is to so grace our children's lives that they are beautifully dressed with wisdom and knowledge as they go out into life. We are not to send them away shamefully unprepared to begin lives away from home. We must rear children who are confident and wise in God's counsel. They should be thoroughly prepared *in* the home for life outside our homes. The beauty of that training, like a gold chain, will be evident to the world into which they enter.

Solomon's cry, "Hear, ye children...," at the start of chapter four becomes a general call for children everywhere to "hear the instruction of a father." How then may they obey if the fathers are not teaching? How is it exactly that we fathers excuse ourselves from these most critical duties? The fact is that most of us fathers and mothers are not teaching our children. This work is often surrendered to others. Typically, what education is provided is such that God is treated as irrelevant or non-existent. We fathers have not accepted the mantle of responsibility to be teachers of our children. In many cases we have not given any serious thought to the implications of this concept. Often we have not even made a simple list of exactly what we want our children to know when they leave our homes. Those that have carefully planned their children's education, and then implemented that plan at home, are as rare as bullfrogs with beards.

Fathers! We have to take the command to teach our children as being for us and for this time. The God we serve, the church, and our families are waiting for us to lead. We are the ones called to teach our children. Our wives are also called to the work but fathers are to lead. It is imperative that we take our children back from the educational institutions and begin doing the work at home. This is one of those ancient paths in which we are called to walk (Jeremiah 6:16).

The commands for God's people to teach their children were given early enough and in sufficient detail that there should be no argument concerning this issue from any of His redeemed today. The foundations for proper education were constructed under the covenantal dispensation of the Old Testament. However, it is useful to note how the New Testament holds to the same ideals concerning education as the Old Testament.

> **And, ye fathers, provoke not your children to wrath: but bring them up in the nurture and admonition of the Lord**
>
> **Ephesians 6:4**

We understand from the Old Testament passages at which we have looked, that bringing up children in the nurture and admonition of the Lord requires much more than just a little Sunday school. Some quick devotions on occasion will not suffice to fulfill the commands God has given us. This Scripture from Paul's letter to the Ephesians is expansive concerning the parents educational duties. The primary responsibility lies with the father first, just as in the Old Testament; "Fathers...bring them up..." It includes all areas of life and knowledge. A Biblical view has to be brought into all teaching. This is the only method that produces children that think Biblically. Bringing up children in the Lord is a work that requires attention in every detail. We are not allowed to rear partly Christian, partly pagan children. They are to be thoroughly Christian.

Bringing them up in the nurture and admonition of the Lord is to be our foremost goal in training the children God gives us. The term "nurture and admonition of the Lord" is not intended to communicate religious instruction while leaving the balance of knowledge to be taught by others. In fact the word nurture indicates personal care, teaching by example, and involvement in the life of the one being taught. Admonition speaks of dealing with attitudes and behavior. Both must receive attention from the teacher to conform the details of the lives of their children to the ways of Christ.

As Christian parents we have to be working to instruct the whole person not just the knowledge base of the child. We cannot underestimate the importance of doing this work God's way. His word is clear. Therefore we must choose to resist the culture and teach our children according to Biblical principle. This is the way of life for our children and families.

# CHAPTER 2

# To Impart a Biblical Worldview

---

"Behold, they have rejected the word of the Lord;
So what wisdom do they have?"

**Jeremiah 8:9  NKJV**

"For I have not shunned to declare unto you all the
counsel of God"

**Acts 20:27**

"...bringing into captivity every thought to the
obedience of Christ"

**2 Corinthians 10:5**

"Beware lest any man spoil you through
philosophy and vain deceit, after the tradition of
men, after the rudiments of the world, and not after
Christ"

**Colossians 2:8**

Jesus told his disciples, "He that is not with me is against me;
and he that gathereth not with me scattereth abroad" (Matthew 12:

30). This teaching defines the distinctive lines of battle as promoted by our Savior. Jesus left no room for equivocating. Political correctness or playing to the crowd were not His styles. Neither should they be ours. Getting along is convenient but it is not always God's will. Faithful Christians often have to choose between approval from the world and approval from God. For many this is a difficult choice. Some begin obedience early while others struggle through a lifetime taking a small step forward and then turning back as soon as the world system applies some pressure to return to its fold.

Here we will discuss what it means to have a Biblical worldview. I will provide examples as to how that works out in a few fields of study. The intention is to give the reader a clear understanding as to the importance of teaching and learning all studies from a Biblical perspective.

Many parents believe that most school studies involve the teaching of much neutral material. Consequently they also believe they can allow their children to be taught from most any text books or from any perspective, just so long as the parents bring in a little Scripture as a balance somewhere along the way. This misunderstanding has brought spiritual destruction to countless Christian children and their families. The damage spreads over generations. Parents often do not understand what happened to their children's faith long after the school years are past.

## THE MYTH OF NEUTRALITY

The idea that neutrality may exist in any classroom is an evil illusion. It attempts to create a middle ground between the kingdom of God and the kingdom of man. Jesus has told us there is no middle ground. In all areas of our existence we are either for Him or against Him. Nothing else exists. The problem then is in our seeing, or lack of seeing, the lines of battle accurately. The apostle Paul explains the authority of Christ to the Colossian church like this:

For by him were all things created, that are in heaven, and that are in earth, visible and invisible, whether they be thrones, or dominions, or principalities, or powers: all things were created by him, and for him: And he is before all things, and by him all things consist. And he is the head of the body, the church: who is the beginning, the firstborn from the dead: that in all things he might have preeminence. And, having made peace through the blood of his cross, by him to reconcile all things unto himself: by him, I say, whether they be things in earth, or things in heaven.

**Colossians 1:16–20**

When Paul teaches that, "all things were created by him, and for him..." and "that in all things he might have preeminence," this leaves no room for the possibility of neutrality. Jesus has not agreed that some parts of life or study may be less than distinctive in honoring Him. Paul emphasizes his point in Colossians 2:2–3 saying:

...their hearts might be comforted, being knit together in love, and unto all riches of the full assurance of understanding, to the acknowledgement of the mystery of God, and of the Father, and of Christ; In whom are hid all the treasures of wisdom and knowledge.

It is these treasures of wisdom and knowledge we seek to impart to our children. If our children are going to attain the "full assurance of understanding" that Paul tells us is the goal, we have to inculcate "the acknowledgement of the mystery of God" in everything we teach. The sinful mind of man always seeks to take steps away from this truth. As we do so our message is quickly lost. Alternative ideas rush in, agreeing with the world that God is irrelevant to what we are doing. This silence of the truth brings ruin for our children and our churches. Silence is not neutral. It is, rather, a vote for the doctrines of man and a dethroning of the doctrines of God. The acceptance of the myth of neutrality is an alliance with the enemies of our faith.

Recently my wife and I attended a seminar introducing the *K12* curriculum promoted by Bill Bennett. We sat politely listening along with a group of Christian homeschool leaders. There was an opportunity before the session to review typical materials from the curriculum. Like us, the others had perused them and found that they taught nothing about the work of God in history or other topics. I personally read one book on George Washington and found an entire lack of mention about the importance of the Christian faith as pertained to his life. During the session the attendees began to insist that these books were not suitable for Christian curriculum due to this writing out of Godly content. So what did our seminar leader try to assert? He began with, "But if the subject is math...", to which a man who had written a Biblically based math program protested instantly that math is not neutral. Then came the reply that surely Christian parents could supplement the materials with Christian teaching! But his arguments were falling on ears of parents who had thought this through for years. They explained to him that materials that write God out of the content are already compromised, and are teaching a different worldview. Christians are not to add God into the larger world of truth. Rather we are to start with God and Jesus Christ who is the truth (John 1), and develop our understanding from that basis. Our study begins with the divine Person and proceeds from there to other topics.

## THE SOVEREIGNTY OF GOD

The real issue we press is the recognition of the sovereignty of God. Does God have all authority in heaven and on earth? Jesus claimed this was so saying, "All power is given unto me in heaven and in earth" (Matthew 28:18). It is the idea that he reigns supreme "in earth" that seems to miss our attention. No believing Christian doubts that Jesus has all power in heaven. We expect Him to rule there. It is His rule on earth that we so easily step past. Some people have argued that the prince of this world is Satan. This is Biblically sound but they forget that Jesus is still king! The king rules and the prince does as he is allowed by the king.

We should never accept defeat by the prince of this world. We may rather expect victory through Christ.

> Behold! My Servant whom I have chosen,
> My Beloved in whom My soul is well pleased!
> I will put My Spirit upon Him,
> And He will declare justice to the Gentiles.
> He will not quarrel or cry out,
> Nor will anyone hear His voice in the streets.
> A bruised reed he will not break,
> And a smoking flax He will not quench,
> Till He sends forth justice to victory;
> And in His name Gentiles will trust.

**Matthew 12:18–21**

We should expect that the Gentiles will trust in Him and that He will send forth justice to victory. The battle is not nearly over and we have no right to concede the field to the enemies of the church. Jesus is still Lord and we are to be advancing His crown rights in every area of inquiry. When we accept the concept that curriculum that writes God out may be acceptable for our children, we have rejected God's sovereign rule in the school. We have agreed with the world that knowledge stands free of the Creator. Therefore, in their thinking, He is an imposition on the curriculum. This is why those who are opposed to Godly obedience sincerely believe we are adding in an unwarranted religion or religious view when we try to mention Jesus in the secular classroom. They do not recognize a sovereign God over all things and so He is foreign to their system. However, in defense of truth we may ask the question in reverse. Why are you (the humanists in control) writing God out of everything being taught? Is this not an attack on the truth? Why do Christians assume that the norm should be to think and study from the perspective of the unbelieving world? We have been deceived. That deception begins with the disposal of a solid belief in the sovereignty of God in the affairs of men. We must return to a correct theology if we are to advance in this battle. When we remove God from the curriculum it is a denial of His sovereignty.

## GOD IS NOT IRRELEVANT

In the government schools, and in many Christian schools, the main message taught is 'the irrelevancy of God in all studies.' No one says this out loud, of course. However, it is the unsaid assumption that underlies every book and curriculum. The non-Christian schools automatically purchase materials that say nothing about the Creator in their texts. For government schools it is the understood norm that God is not to be mentioned in the classroom. The Christian schools often purchase similar books, sometimes obtaining them from government sources. There may be occasions throughout the year when the teacher attempts to build thought about God into the studies, but this is not normative. It is not unusual for the Christian teacher to open the class with prayer and then never mention God in relation to the studies at hand. Some Christian teachers do better than this but many do not. They have never been taught from a Biblical perspective in what they teach and so do not know there is anything missing from their curriculum.

This issue of the irrelevancy of God in the school is no small problem. By excluding God from the study materials, the school teaches by its example that God is not of sufficient importance to be discussed. That attitude is imparted directly to the students who then see nothing wrong with that attitude since it is just normal to them. They think of discussions about God and His providence as irrelevant to what is done at the institution. It is a belief that carries on throughout their lives even though it has never been seriously considered.

Both of my daughters attended conservative Christian colleges, one of which was a Bible college. Both girls were disappointed with the lack of Biblical content in the classrooms. I interviewed the head of the department where my oldest daughter was majoring and was assured that every class was taught from a Christian worldview. The instructor had supposedly been put through a twenty hour class on teaching from a Biblical worldview and would use that training in her instruction. The reports I received from my daughter were that in most of the classes the instructors said exactly nothing about Christian thought as relates to the discipline.

I have talked to parents from across the country concerning this issue. The reports I receive are almost all similar. The Christian college literature all promises that the schools promote a Christian worldview approach to their studies. In reality the colleges hardly ever deliver. My younger daughter faced this same difficulty at the Christian college she attended in northern Minnesota. In her history classes, psychology class or in any non-Bible class, God was rarely if ever mentioned. His providence was not discussed in the history classes, ever. When I wrote to the psychology professor complaining about the failure to teach Biblical thought he wrote back to me saying, "I taught the content of the discipline" and "it was not a theology class." Of course that begged the question, Did you show the student how the mind of God relates to this field of study? Their answer was a resounding no, and that quite defensively. My question now is, then why do we need you? Why do Christian parents need Christian schools that do not teach Christian thought? If God is irrelevant to the studies why do we need the schools? I am convinced that the problems we have seen at the college level through our own family are nearly as persistent at the grade school and high school levels as well (there are notable exceptions with schools that have adopted a Principle Approach). The reports we have received from Christian parents typically confirm this. Often the class sessions open with prayer but the teaching has nothing to say about God in relation to the curriculum content. The irrelevancy of God problem pervades both public and private schools, and will not be fixed in the foreseeable future. If God's direct commands for parents to teach their children are not sufficient, this additional disaster should give parents further pause to consider removing them from the schools.

## THE TEACHING CONTEXT

Many Christian parents (and teachers as well) continue to be pulled along with the thinking that most school subjects are pretty much neutral. Knowledge is knowledge they say. What difference the source, just so long as the facts are taught?

The idea that the "facts" are being taught is an unlikely assumption, as other authors have demonstrated.[1] The facts about history, social studies, arts, even math, are not being presented to our students in a great many cases.

But, the issue we will look at first is the context in which information is being transmitted. Education is much more than the inculcating of knowledge. When knowledge is imparted it is always delivered in a philosophical context. It is this context about which we need to be cognizant.

When a teacher selects a textbook or curriculum the materials invariably carry the author's philosophical perspective. Every writer has a view of the world, and that view will automatically be worked into whatever work that writer produces. It is inevitable. Therefore, no material will be neutral. The meaning of what is being presented will be interpreted by the author and be made an integral part of the work. This begins with the selection of materials placed in the book —what is important? And what may be left out? Those decisions affect directly the facts that will be taught. They also teach by example what is important to discuss in school and what is not important to discuss. So, just at this base level of constructing a curriculum we can see that there is no neutrality. The facts presented are those thought important by the curriculum writer.

For example, one history textbook may spend a great deal of space discussing foundational documents and their original meaning. A similar text may eliminate discussion of all such documents, thus communicating that those writings are not essential learning.

This book is too small to delve deeply into the details of what it means to teach from a Biblical worldview. We will take some effort though, to demonstrate how a few authors reveal their worldview through what is in their texts. Hopefully this will give the reader some useful suggestions as to how to identify the mind-set reflected in the materials his children are using. I found it eye popping to discover such clear statements of philosophy and purpose in textbooks when I first began these studies.

## ENCYCLOPEDIA NOT NEUTRAL

As I started my research for this chapter I went to our local library and began pulling books I believed would give some clear statements as to the author's intent. As I walked through the section devoted to younger readers I spied the *Academic American Encyclopedia,* Volume 1, A–Ang came to hand. The introduction gave the author's intentions in multiple paragraphs. Many were good and necessary, and pretty much everybody could agree with the statements. But consider this statement under the section titled Objectivity:

> A concerted effort has been made to produce an encyclopedia free of sexist language and attitudes, although that task is especially difficult in certain articles in philosophy and religion, where writers before the 20th century commonly used "man" in both a generic and a literal sense.[2]

What we are seeing here is the author's bias against the Biblically based use of language as regards the sexes. The Bible calls our race *man*. God did not leave the term or its meaning up for further definition. Yet this encyclopedia has taken on the enormous task of eviscerating the term and its attendant meaning from its text. This means that opposing language and ideas, have to be generated to replace what has been the normal Christian word usage for thousands of years. It is an attempt to redefine the patriarchal view from the Scriptures with a different cultural concept. The author has defined the historic Biblical idea as sexist while introducing his new philosophy with no name. We are to believe his new idea is just normal. No reason is given as to why the historic patriarchal concept is wrong; it just is, in this book. Notice the author's reference to "certain articles in philosophy and religion." These are the root of the problem, are they not? It was those Christian philosophers and religionists who kept imitating the Bible in its use of the male prerogative.

This may not seem like much to some readers but it was highly important to the writers of the text. It was of sufficient import to justify the work put into changing the book's language and in informing us of the change. This is because the author understands there are tremendous implications connected to this rearrangement of words. He believes that by denying male headship within the language he undermines the Biblical doctrine of patriarchy. He changes the perceived roles of male and female away from the Biblical model and points them in a different direction. It is subtle but effective. The author(s) have a philosophical and ultimately religious perspective they want to communicate. This is one way of accomplishing that task. Consequently, let the reader (or his children) beware this text. It teaches heresy by its very construction. Christian children should not be educated from materials with this type of philosophy built in.

Lest the reader think that I am whipping up a frenzy over the rare misstep of our schoolbook writing friends we will examine several more examples. This same encyclopedia book contains a large section on the American War for Independence. I looked in vain for any mention of the providence of God in that war. It said nothing about the obvious providential works of God against the British at the battle of Yorktown. Instead the author attributed the destruction of Cornwallis's army to the British "failure to recognize the significance of sea power."[3] Besides being an unforgivable distortion of the facts, this treatment circumvents the obvious miracles of the time and purposefully disposes of the discussions the patriots of the day had about the salvation of the Lord in their time.

The text equally mangles George Washington's army's escape from New York in September 1776, saying only that he was "hopelessly outflanked"[4] and mentioning nothing about the miraculous fog that allowed Washington to remove his entire army to safety in such an unprecedented manner. Washington and his men related the event as directly from the hand of God, but this author cares nothing for the view of the men that were there. The reader will not learn of the providence of God in New York from this author, although it was a signal event in the forming of our nation. There is not a single word about God's providence in the War for Independence in this encyclopedia.

Sometimes authors tell us when they are out to destroy Christian ideals and other times they just go ahead and write from their own non-Christian mind. Either way, Christian students will be inculcated with thought that opposes truth and the Christian tradition. There is simply no way for parents to protect their children from these kinds of influences when the children are away in schools for most of the day. And protecting our children is really just a mild first step. The goal is not to just protect, it is to train in Biblical thought in every subject area. This goal is much more aggressive. It means we are not satisfied to correct the high points. Rather we are to build them up in the nurture and admonition of the Lord in all that is taught. The entire curriculum is to be directed toward truth and high-minded Biblical ideals. We do not want to supplement the curriculum with Jesus. The curriculum is Jesus first and foremost, with other knowledge taught in its relationship to the Creator.

# INTEGRATION OF SCRIPTURE FAILS

Many schools advertise that they integrate Christian thought into their teaching. When the schools integrated the races a few decades back it meant that the schools still were basically white but that black students could be added to what was there already. No one challenged the foundational precept that the schools were dominated by white students and white culture. I am making no judgment about that fact but I am pointing out that we are doing the same type of thing when we integrate Christian thought into a school. We are agreeing that the true base for knowledge is something outside our Biblical tradition and that spiritual things are going to be added to that predominant base. This reflects a false theory of knowledge. It is a theory that begins with man, or the thoughts of man, and tries to build from there. It is a mistaken foundation. Rather, Christians must begin with God and then determine how all learning relates to Him and His purposes. The beauty of His character is to be noted and communicated through what is known. The message of the universe is not primarily about man. It is about God. We pursue knowledge in order to glorify God and serve man. We desire knowledge but we regard God more highly than our accumulation of that knowledge. Everything begins and finishes with Him.

When we see Christian schools advertising that they integrate the Bible into their studies we now assume that the school officials really have no understanding of what it means to teach from a Biblical worldview. Integration is a flawed concept from its outset. Christian students should flee these schools. If they remain they will only become confused by the contradictions built into the teaching. To integrate Godly thought into a man centered curriculum is impossible. God does not conform His word or His work to fit man's contemplations. Rather, we must fit ours to His. This flawed theory of knowledge called integration carries no value for the Christian student. It is another reason parents should obey God and teach their own children. The parents can start with a correct base at the outset.

# ANTI-GOD SCHOOLS AND HISTORIES

"All of life is an experiment. Every year if not every day we have to wager our salvation upon some prophecy based upon imperfect knowledge."[5] So says Oliver Wendell Holmes, Jr. as quoted in *The Americans – The Democratic Experience*. This book by Daniel Boorstin is typical of the history books from which students will study in either government or private schools. Boorstin is a popular historian. He has done much fine research. However, as Christian parents we have to be thinking about the worldview promoted in the materials we use to teach our children.

Would we, for instance, really want our children to be taught that, "All of life is an experiment"? and that, "we have to wager our salvation" as the above quote indicates?

These types of statements are not innocent. They teach not just a wrong philosophy but an incorrect theology. They are given as building blocks for life. In this case the book is a history book but the quote from Holmes is not about historical data. It is about salvation, prophecy and epistemology. Boorstin understands that the study of history interconnects with all other fields of inquiry. The problem for us as Christian parents is that we do not understand this basic tenet. We have acted as if we can expect to separate the subject areas, teaching spiritual things as an add-on to other *neutral* material. The opponents to our faith know otherwise and work daily to press the battle to their advantage.

Our Christian naiveté was evident to Boorstin as he wrote in this same chapter (titled *Prologue to Foreign Aid*) about the advancement of education at the turn of the nineteenth century saying, "Education, which was becoming a secular religion within the United States, became an agency of missions abroad. American missionaries carried this gospel of education to the farthest corners of the world." So in Boorstin's estimation it was American, Christian missionaries who spread the idea of the secular education system around the world. American missionaries were not the originators of this problem but they were the ones who promoted secularized education world wide.

The intention here is not to attack American missionaries. The point is that by the turn of the nineteenth century the American church had been completely captured by the idea that most knowledge and teaching are neutral. This concept had invaded our schools and had been accepted by almost everyone. Even the church leaders had been drawn in. Now as we are faced with the results of over a century of this practice we need to rethink the first premise. Can Christian education be given or received using materials that do not specifically inculcate Biblical thought? Can the teacher or the curriculum be neutral? The answer is clearly NO. This is why the discussion about worldview or Biblical view is so important. Our children do not just need to be educated. They need to be taught the Christian faith as a complete system in all subject areas. When we do this we will end up with children that are distinctively Christian. This should be our goal.

## THE ATTACK ON LANGUAGE

One aspect of the Biblical view, or worldview battle, that has been underway for almost two centuries has to do with the English language itself. The attack on Christian civilization was fought and won by anti-Christian publishers in the area of linguistics, prior to the year 1900. The victory is so complete that very few Christians know about the struggles that went on before the turn of that century.

It was Noah Webster who wrote the first truly American Dictionary, and it was built on solid Christian principle. Prior to Webster the most used English dictionary was a volume by Samuel Johnson published in 1755. What Noah Webster did was to introduce superior scholarship in researching the etymology of the words, and he also built his definitions using Biblical examples. He then went on to eliminate vulgar words explaining:

It is questionable how far vulgar and cant words are to be admitted into a dictionary; but one thing must be acknowledged by any man who will inspect the several dictionaries of the English language...Johnson has transgressed the rules of lexicography beyond any compiler; for his work contains more of the lowest of all vulgar words than any other now extant...Any person who will have the patience and the candor to compare my dictionary with others will find that there is not a vocabulary of the English language extant so free from local, vulgar, and obscene words as mine!...[6]

Webster's theology led him to create a dictionary that eliminated vulgar words because he believed that his work should direct Christian culture toward nobler ideals. He knew that by eliminating those words from his dictionary he delegitimized them, which would lead to their disuse. Webster's work therefore carried a moral concern that was designed to push forward Christian civilization. His Biblical worldview was reflected in his work.

There were other important aspects built into this dictionary. Rosalie J. Slater writes:

Noah Webster's 1828 American Dictionary remains today the pure repository of three essential ingredients of America's Christian History. It reflects our Christian philosophy of life, our Christian philosophy of government, and our Christian philosophy of education. Unmistakably it reveals the degree to which the Bible was America's basic textbook and how it was related to all fields. Noah Webster as a Christian scholar laid his foundation of etymology upon the Scriptures and his research into the origin of language stems from this premise. One cannot read his definitions nor study his discussion of the grammatical construction of our language without encountering at every point a Scriptural Christian philosophy of life.[7]

Webster was the first to so thoroughly build a dictionary based upon Christian principle. His dictionary became the measure of the language for decades to come. It helped secure Christian thought as normal for the nation. Of course there were many destructive influences working on American civilization during the 1800s but Webster's dictionary had a great and positive effect. It helped define the Christian worldview as being American and as the standard for our people. By carrying Biblical thought about life, government, and education into his definitions he helped thousands of people develop a Biblical worldview. Our nation is indebted to Webster for his contributions to our spiritual heritage. Excellent Christian theology had been inserted directly into the language itself.

Webster passed from the scene and the nineteenth century progressed. After the death of Noah Webster the field of linguistics began to be dominated by scholars with a more humanistic perspective. Their desire was to eliminate the Biblical thought Webster had brought forward and replace it with works that reflected their own perspective. When their dictionary first came out in the late nineteenth century it was the subject of great public debate. Newspaper headlines announced the struggle between the new and the old (Webster's 1828). Scholars understood that the ones that define the words of the culture also define the theology of the culture. They establish the base line from which much thought within the society is deduced. The victor in the battle for linguistics carries forward an advantage that will affect all future discussions within the society. Daniel Boorstin describes it this way:

> By the mid-twentieth century, new democratic criteria had come into the classroom, changing the notion of what standards, if any, a democratic society could apply to its language. These were the product of a new science of linguistics. Until about the mid-nineteenth century, studies of the origin and development of language had been tangled with theology, philosophy, rhetoric, and logic.[8]

30

These "democratic criteria," e.g. humanistic ideals, have now become the norm as the philosophical underpinning for American English. This condition makes it only more difficult to inculcate Christian thought in our children. It means that in the struggle to impart a Biblical mind in our students we have to go right to the root in everything. Parents may do this at home as a conscious effort to teach Christianity to their offspring. This kind of effort will almost never be attempted at any modern school. How deep does the rabbit hole go? It goes to the roots of the language. Christians have a great deal of work to do to recapture this culture for Christ. This is a part of the struggle to resurrect a Biblical worldview within this society.

## WORLDVIEW IN ART TEXTBOOKS

The hostility toward Christian faith now permeates textbooks in the schools. While parents imagine that the schools are neutral, the fact is that a non-Christian religion of Humanism or sometimes even open paganism underlies most of the curriculum. Often times the author's philosophy is very easy to identify. They are forthright in letting the reader know what they believe. It was quite easy for me to glean numbers of these quotes in a single afternoon at the local library.

Perusing an artistic photography book of the Himalayas I found a long quote by Arnold Toynbee in the foreword. Consider these few lines from his longer text:

> ...The splendor that shines through Nature is imparted to her from a source which is beyond Nature and which is the ultimate reality... As I flew over the Himalayas...For a moment, Nature seemed more powerful than even modern Man...Since Man became conscious, he has been aware that he himself is not the spiritually highest presence in the universe, and he has been seeking to communicate with this higher form of reality in order to put himself into harmony

with it...At the western end of the Old World and in the Americas this earliest form of religion has been killed by monotheism in the forms of Judaism, Christianity, and Islam. But in India and Eastern Asia the worship of ultimate reality through the medium of nature still survives. [Capitalization as in original][9]

This art book makes no effort to hide its intent. The reader is supposed to reject the God of the west and turn to the gods of Nature while reviewing the photos. There is nothing neutral here, but simply the worship of creation rather than the Creator. But if your child were using this book in an art class at school, would you even know what he was being taught or would you just see nice pictures in a beautiful book? These kinds of texts and teaching fly right past most parents as Johnny and Suzie pass through an educational system thought to be neutral by Mom and Dad.

The fact that culture is communicated in every subject area in the schools is common knowledge outside of the Christian cultural ghetto. Think about this quote from a sixty year old art book titled, *Modern American Painting.*

In America, the artist has once again accomplished his historical mission—for Art is the cultural expression of the human race in visual terms, just as, by the same token, Science is the culture of a people expressed in terms of applied experiment to the how of things, and Philosophy is a culture expressed in terms of reasoning into the why of things. Music fills the same function in terms of sound, and Literature in terms of the written language.[10]

In the field of art the battle rages against Christian thought almost everywhere we look. Modern art is the retracement of thought back before the garden. At the beginning of creation the Scriptures tell us that, "the earth was without form and void." Yet before that first day had passed, God "divided the light from the darkness," thus beginning to create form. During the following days He filled the void with every type of beauty.

Modern art rejects the ideas about form and beauty put forward by God Himself. Rather, it seeks to return the world to a place "without form and void." It is void of any worthy moral direction. It is void of beauty. Form, line, and categories, required to depict Biblical thought have been erased. Therefore we reject modern art not because of any fault with the media but because the message is false and its morality perverse.

As the quote from *Modern American Painting* tells us, "the artist has once again accomplished his historical mission;" and in fact gone beyond the historical mission of expressing the values of the culture to directing the values of the culture. The older schools of art depicted a sacred creation. Modern artists depict their own work (and thus themselves) as sacred. A different theology is reflected. The world has not changed but their perception of it has.

Take notice as to how the above quote from *Modern American Painting* demonstrates the connectedness of all fields of inquiry. Philosophy, science, art, and music are all understood to be expressions of a culture. Somehow, Christians have come to believe that Christianity encompasses only a few thoughts about personal piety and evangelism. Meanwhile the larger culture is moved toward anti-Christian ideas by those who have a more complete view of the world. Biblical concepts have been eradicated from the public square in almost every field. Now the culture is beginning to turn its attention toward the last two areas of resistance within Christianity, morals and evangelism. These two last bastions of the faith are under attack with evangelistic talk, or preaching against the homosexual life style being depicted as hate speech. Yet somehow many Christians believe they can avoid confronting the culture and just stay safe in their churches. Sending their children to government schools to be taught the cultural myths of the age is seemingly no problem for these parents.

In this chapter I have given examples from history, linguistics, and art. This is merely a beginning in the worldview discussion. The same conversation could be continued in the fields of biology, math, geography, government, or any other topic area. There is not room here to delve into detail in any of these. However, the Christian curriculum must be constructed to recognize the mind of God in all of these and more. It is the work of parents to teach their children in this way. The task is challenging but not impossible.

In the book of Ezekiel chapter forty-four verse twenty-three, God commands His priests that, "they shall teach my people the difference between the holy and profane, and cause them to discern between the unclean and the clean." Once again the church leadership is called to teach the people of God to discern in this way. What is the difference between the holy and the profane? In many areas the church has forgotten. Renewal will come when the churches preach truth and the parents teach it to their children. We must stop rearing profane children. God has given us a better hope.

## CHAPTER 3

# It is the Only Method God Allows

And turn ye not aside: for then should ye go after
vain things, which cannot profit nor deliver; for
they are vain.

**1 Samuel 12:21**

When we discuss the Scriptures and the will of God concerning homeschooling we are often told by parents that their duty to educate their child is to be understood as a responsibility to make sure the child gets educated. They say the means is not the issue. The important thing is that the parents do not let the child grow up uneducated. So under this view (which is altogether common), the parents are obeying God's commands to teach their children by delegating the work to a school. Parents that are a little more wealthy, or concerned for their child's welfare, may delegate the work to a private school rather than a public institution. Either way, the case is argued that delegation of educational duties is a legitimate means of obedience for parents to train their children. This chapter will refute that view with Biblical examples and Biblical reasoning.

# WHERE AUTHORITY COMES FROM

As we begin to consider this question about who God allows to teach our children we quickly discover that it is fundamentally a matter of deciding who has authority to teach them. Generally speaking, most Christian parents have never addressed this from the Scriptures. They are assuming that children may be taught by most anyone the parent or school appoints. For many parents this is an uninvestigated belief. It has never been measured against Biblical standards.

Any discussion of authority has to start with God. He is the One who spoke everything into being. He created all things and then set them in order according to His perfect will. The earth rotates due to His sustaining power. The sun crosses the heavens by His guidance (Psalm 19). He rules the nations (Psalm 2), determines the outcome of wars (Psalm 46:9), raises up nations and turns the hearts of kings (Proverbs 21:1). Everywhere His power and authority are made evident. So when Jesus told His disciples, "All authority is given unto Me in heaven and on earth," (Matthew 28:18) it was a claim intended to be taken with the same trembling as the words to Moses, "I Am that I Am." Jesus was not announcing useless information. He was giving us a key to understanding His position in the Godhead and the continuity of the Old and New Testaments. The authority of Jehovah was the authority of Christ. The Father had given Him authority over all things, not only in heaven but on earth. Questions about authority do not relate only to the heavenly order. They extend to dealings on earth since the earth is rightly under His dominion.

How God wants authority over education exercised on earth, is the question we must answer. The will of God concerning authority is not secret. Rather, He has given us His precepts (His preceptive will) for guidance in our duties. Our work is to discover that will and do it.

# WHAT ARE THE OPTIONS?

The commands to teach children are given to parents in both testaments. None are given to civil authority or to the church (more on that later). When we talk about the authority to teach children, and its possible delegation to someone other than the parents, we have only a few potential courses of action.

1. We may assert that when the Bible gives commands for actions, that it normally allows for delegation of those duties. In other words it would be common to find, within the Biblical text, examples of God's people who righteously delegated duties specifically assigned to them by God.

2. We could try to show that the mandate for parents to teach their children is a special case, which, as such, may be delegated to others.

3. We can accept the charge God has given as a direct responsibility of the parents.

Choice number one requires an expansive view of the Biblical text. It says that if we just look through God's many commands to individuals we will see how those duties are normally delegated to second or third parties, and that God is pleased with that behavior. So we begin our search, but what do we find? When God told Moses to go and speak to Pharaoh, Moses balked, saying he was not a good speaker (Exodus 4:10, Moses fibbed—see Acts 7:22). God allowed Aaron to speak to Pharaoh for Moses, but only after expressing His anger at Moses' intransigence (Exodus 4:14). In the end Moses spoke to Pharaoh directly (Exodus 8:9), thus fulfilling the revealed will of God. Jehovah allowed a secondary method but it was clearly not His desire to use Aaron. Moses was supposed to do the speaking. God's first choice was the best choice as we can see from the later texts. We are not to imitate the mistake that Moses made.

We may look at Saul's experience on his return from his battle with the Amalekites in 1 Samuel 15. He (Israel) had been commanded to "slay both man and woman, infant and suckling, ox and sheep, camel and ass" (Verse 3). During the battle Saul "took Agag the king of the Amalekites alive" (verse 8). The prophet Samuel upon discovering Saul's disobedience "hewed Agag in pieces before the Lord in Gilgal" (verse 33). The prophet did the work God had sent Saul to do. Due to Saul's failure to do God's will directly, Samuel told him "for thou hast rejected the word of the Lord, and the Lord hath rejected thee from being king over Israel" (verse 26). Saul's alternate plan was not acceptable to God. Even though he pleaded for pardon he never recovered God's blessing over his office as king.

Consider David, whose office it was to lead his army. 2 Samuel 11:1 tells us "And it came to pass...at the time when kings go forth to battle, that David sent Joab, and his servants with him...But David tarried still at Jerusalem." It seemed such a small thing for David to send Joab to stand in for the king. After all, Joab was an experienced warrior, why not delegate the authority this one season? Other kings went to battle but not David. Instead he sent Joab and this leads to David's downfall with Bathsheba and the murder of her husband. The results nearly destroyed David as king. David should have been in the field with his men. The leader needed to lead but by giving his duties to another he opened the door for murder and adultery. There are some duties we should never delegate.

I have been unable to find any rule of interpretation or any example in the Scriptures that would lend credence to the idea that the obedience God demands from individuals or families may be delegated to others. When I investigate examples of this type of delegation of authority it only leads to sin and compounded problems. The duties God has specifically given us are not to be handed over to someone else. When we disobey God in this way it leads only to sin and God's judgment. A decision to delegate authority outside of God's will is an attempt to dethrone the Creator and place man on the throne. It is the insistence that man is wiser than his Maker. Man, once again, picks the forbidden fruit.

Does this mean that Christians are *never* to delegate authority? No it does not, but it does mean we may only delegate authority such as

God commands. Examples would be Titus being told to ordain elders in every city to rule the churches (Titus 1:5), or Moses appointing judges over tens, fifties, hundreds, and thousands (Deuteronomy 1: 15 ff). The concept of delegating authority is a good thing. However, it is God's prerogative to direct His authority, *not man's*. When man delegates authority it must be done at God's command and consonant with His revealed will. There is no command or example in Scripture for parents to delegate education to schools.

Some will argue that the education of children represents a special case, as I mentioned in choice number two above. The idea is that these particular commands by God, for parents to educate their children, are not like other commands He makes. Surely we cannot expect parents in this complex world to teach their own children! Allowances must be made for the realities of life! How can anyone be so narrow as to think God still demands this same behavior? And so the arguments go. However, none of these are Biblically based. The question stands: what exactly is the Biblical basis to say that God's commands concerning education are to be treated as a special case, to be delegated whenever desired? My contention is that there is no such special rule of interpretation for these decrees of God.

## WHAT ABOUT EXCEPTIONS?

We do have a *seeming* exception to the rule as found with Hannah and her son Samuel. The story is found in the first chapter of 1 Samuel. Hannah, having been married for some time, is found without child. God had promised His people that if they were faithful He would give them children as a part of His covenant promise (Deuteronomy 7:14). Hannah was not experiencing that covenant faithfulness and was being mocked by her husband's other wife (1 Samuel 1:6). Being grieved, Hannah vows to God that if He will give her a son she will dedicate that son to His service (verse 11). The priest Eli notices she is troubled and then prays for her request to be answered (verse 17). Her desire is granted and she brings Samuel to the care of Eli the priest as soon as her son is weaned.

The case of Hannah is special because her son is the unusual answer to prayer by both herself and a Levitical priest. Notice also that Hannah had dedicated her son to the Lord before he was conceived promising that, "There shall no razor come upon his head" (verse 11), possibly indicating a Nazaritic dedication. The event was clearly engineered by God to bring the prophet Samuel to the priesthood at an appointed time when the first king of Israel, Saul, was established. This was not a normal event in Israel. It was the exception to every rule and was a special work by God in a life that was to be marked by historic events. We cannot make this single instance the measure for our families. This story does not abrogate the clear commands of God concerning the education of our children.

The conclusion of the matter is this: that God has not granted families the authority to sublet the education of their children to others. The normal, Scriptural, pattern is for parents to teach their own children. This is the beginning of wisdom in education.

## THE ARGUMENT FROM SILENCE

There are other arguments made in attempts to bypass the direction God has given. Many will argue that there are no Scriptures forbidding government or private schools. This is true, but it is a classic argument from silence. Where do we ever find the authors of Scripture making this type of argument or interpretation? We do not. The writers of Scripture always construct doctrine based upon what has been revealed. It is impossible to discover good doctrine based on what the Bible does *not* say. The fact that the Bible does not say something proves nothing.

I discussed these issues with a pastor friend some years ago. His response was that the Jewish people had Synagogue schools. He told me it is common knowledge that Jewish people have placed their children in synagogue schools for centuries. Therefore, he concluded, Christians have justification for sending their children off to schools of their choice. This was a clever misdirection of the conversation. It sets aside the Bible as our authority and uses history as the source of faith and practice. This subterfuge may give him a way to ignore God's commands but it will purchase no mercy at the judgment.

## Do Not Be Unequally Yoked

Consider this passage from 2 Corinthians 6:14–18:

> Be ye not unequally yoked together with unbelievers: for what fellowship hath righteousness with unrighteousness? And what communion hath light with darkness? And what concord hath Christ with Belial? Or what part hath he that believeth with an infidel? And what agreement hath the temple of God with idols? for ye are the temple of the living God; as God hath said, I will dwell in them, and walk in them; and I will be their God, and they shall be my people. Wherefore come out from among them, and be ye separate, saith the Lord, and touch not the unclean thing; and I will receive you, and will be a Father unto you, and ye shall be my sons and daughters, saith the Lord Almighty.

The concepts taught here overflow with meaning for us as we discuss the education of our children.

"Be not unequally yoked together with unbelievers," Paul tells us. When oxen are yoked together they travel everywhere together, they eat the same food, they obey the same commands, and accomplish the same work. Yoked oxen walk side by side at the same speed, they recognize the same master, and head for the same destination. Is this not what we do when we place our children in a government school? I believe it is. The sons and daughters of Christian parents ride the same buses, sit in the common classrooms, listen to the same teaching, are taught the same worldview, and absorb the same irreverent attitudes toward God as their unbelieving peers. Nothing could be further from God's will for our children.

"What fellowship hath righteousness with unrighteousness?" we are asked. This talk of righteousness places a moral framework around the question. The first and most important consideration in being unequally yoked is that of righteousness. A morally pure heart does not desire to be closely engaged with unrighteousness or an unrighteous man, woman or child. Christians often turn to this Scripture as a proof that God's people should not marry unbelievers. That is a valid application, but it is not the only application. There is a general principle that says that righteousness cannot dwell successfully with unrighteousness. Righteousness has a fragile quality. This is why Paul tells us that, "Bad company corrupts good morals" (1 Corinthians 15:33). As parents we are required to shelter our children from prolonged, close contact with unrighteous people. As we grow older and more mature we learn fixed habits. We also glean our learning from a variety of sources, including reading the Word. However, children are always learning by example. It is their first source, especially at an early age. To put them in a school surrounded with unrighteous (unregenerate) teachers and peers is folly. Righteousness cannot have fellowship with unrighteousness because they are at war.

Christians often use the Biblical language about light and darkness. We believe there is a grand battle with soldiers of light battling forces of darkness in the heavens. Of course the battle also ranges across the earth but it seems less distinct in our minds. Maybe we see the warfare in a political setting or perhaps when conflict enters the church. Yet as a body we easily dismiss talk of a battle within the schools. It is as if parents are desperately clinging to a hope that the darkness has not engulfed their school. Does unrighteousness really fill that place? Are we not being overly dramatic they ask? But if we inquire "do you believe your local school is a source of Christian righteousness?" the answer is clearly no. So the argument is made.

None of us believe the schools will make our children more righteous. There is a quiet battle between the camps of the light and the darkness as pertains to education. Has that darkness invaded your home and family unnoticed?

Paul asks, "what concord hath Christ with Belial?" The answer is supposed to be none. And yet Christian parents daily imagine that this concern is of no consequence. Notice the sharp division God gives us. We may infer that being yoked with unbelievers is the same as being yoked to Belial—Satan. Remember that the Bible only allows for two camps; the redeemed and the lost, the children of the first Adam and the children of the second Adam, the sons of God and the sons of Belial. How then do we believe that it is acceptable to yoke our children with those of the enemies of Christ? Do the children of light have the same goals as the children of darkness? Do they travel to the same eternal city? Should they learn the same morals, think the same thoughts, or be taught the same worldview? How can we evangelical parents be so confused as to believe these things? Are we asleep, or deceived, or are we immorally choosing to disobey the God of the church?

"What part hath he that believeth with an infidel?" Paul inquires. This should be a consuming question for every believing parent. By what authority does any Christian parent yoke his child to the children of an "infidel"? The unbeliever is to be shown a righteous life and to see Godly families in the community. He is not to be yoked to our children for six hours a day, five days a week, nine months a year, for thirteen years. Do not be fooled by the idea that this is somehow obeying God by witnessing. It is not witnessing, it is yoking, and it is forbidden. I am afraid that in many cases our eyes have been blinded and we barely discern the difference between light and darkness.

The apostle pounds his point deeper saying, "what agreement hath the temple of God with idols? for ye are the temple of the living God." Paul has turned to a deeper truth. We are not just *watching* a battle between Christ and Satan. We *are* the temple of God. All of life is religious. Every deed and thought should be understood as a part of the work God is performing in us. For the Christian all things are sacred. When we compromise our lives or pollute them with the thoughts and works of the unbelievers we are not just messing up ourselves, we are despoiling the very temple of God. It is an abomination to Him, an insult to the Creator, when we yoke His temple to the temple of idols. God assures us we are the temple of God but also recognizes the unbelievers as temples of idols. It is a poignant image; God's high and holy dwelling lashed to the temple of Baal. What spirit is it that fills our minds to believe we may make such sport of His calling and election? Why do we sacrifice our children to the idols of the age? What have we become?

## COME OUT FROM AMONG THEM

"Come out from among them, and be ye separate, saith the Lord, and touch not the unclean thing," is God's call on our lives and the lives of our children. It is impossible to assert that we have "come out from among them" when our children are deeply embedded in their avowedly secular schools. If this call to come out has any meaning at all we need to apply it here. There could be no more clear case. The hearts and minds of children are largely shaped by the environment in which they are placed. The call to "come out from among them" is designed for just such a situation as we have with the government schools today.

God tells us "be ye separate…and I will receive you, and will be a Father unto you, and ye shall be my sons and daughters, saith the Lord Almighty." This final appeal seizes the heart with its gravity and emotion. When we remove our children from under the God ordained family and place them with the enemies of God we are making them as orphans. Their true parents are replaced with new fathers and new mothers who do not know the Lord. They are being discipled and reared by a different family than that in which God placed them. The call to be separate is the call to be the true parents of our children. In response to our obedience God promises to "be a Father unto you." He will be our Provider, and Keeper, Deliverer and Friend. We will be His sons and daughters, looking to Him to fulfill every need and to keep us in His care. Why then do we think that the world and its schools have anything we need? Why do we so aspire to have their approval and their degrees? Have we made our children orphans of heaven? Whose children have they become?

## What About Christian Schools?

Over the past four decades there has been an enormous growth in the building of Christian schools. As parents have seen the increasing wickedness gushing from the government institutions, they are taking a step back to shelter their offspring. In a sense this is a good thing, in that an awakening has begun. However, there are important considerations to address in relation to this growing trend.

It should be observed that there are no Biblical injunctions for the church to educate children. The only commands given are made to the parents, not to the church. Admittedly the church has been given gifted teachers by the Holy Spirit. Presumably those teachers are supposed to be teaching somebody. Bishops are to teach as a function of their office (1 Timothy 3:2). So even though we have no Biblical examples of the church directing educational ministry to children, it may be over-stating the case to say that the church is never to teach children school subjects. We do have Old Testament examples of parents and children being taught together (Joshua 8:35) but this is vastly different than what the church schools are presently doing. The church school is certainly not a Biblical model. It is a model taken from outside the Bible and imposed on the church as an answer to pressing difficulties that we face.

The largest problem that church or private schools have, in common with their government counterparts, is that by necessity the school divorces the child from the family. Institutionalized training by its very nature guarantees that the child will be under the care of someone other than the family for many of the child's waking hours. Correct instruction for our children includes training both the intellect and the heart. We have to teach the whole person, not just the brain. Ethics, personal relationships, practicing giving, kindness, and repentance are all a part of a proper education. These types of learning are inculcated best in the home by parents that love the child. Parents who rightly believe they are called by the Lord to rear Godly children can rear excellent sons and daughters God's way. No school can substitute for a righteous Christian family. We are mistaken when we think that education is primarily about filling the brain with facts. It is much more than that. The best Christian schools are an inadequate substitute for Christian parents.

There is a story recorded in Judges that illustrates the error of substituting something good in violation of God's revealed will. The hero of the account is Gideon, fresh from the successful destruction of the Midianite army. Gideon is the man that grew a crop of wheat and harvested it while the rest of the men of Israel "made them the dens which are in the mountains, and caves, and strongholds" (Judges 6:2). When the angel of the Lord called him to lead the battle against the Midianites the angel addressed Gideon as "thou mighty man of valor" (Judges 6:12). Having freed Israel from the rule of Midian Gideon became highly revered. Our text is Judges 8:22–27:

> Then the men of Israel said to Gideon, Rule thou over us, both thou, and thy son, and thy son's son also: for thou hast delivered us from the hand of Midian. And Gideon said unto them, I will not rule over you, neither shall my son rule over you: the Lord shall rule over you. And Gideon said unto them, I would desire a request of you, that ye would give me every man the earrings of his prey …And they answered, We will willingly give them. And they did spread a garment, and did cast therein every man the earrings of his prey. And the weight of the golden earrings that he requested was a thousand and seven hundred shekels of gold…And Gideon made

an ephod thereof, and put it in his city, even in Ophrah: and all Israel went thither a whoring after it: which thing became a snare unto Gideon, and to his house.

Gideon was a man who started well. He refused to be brought under the unrighteous rule of Midian. Against all odds he planted a field and harvested a crop. When called to battle, by God, he asked for the miracle of the fleece and received the miraculous answer. By the power of God's hand Gideon defeated the enemy. His countrymen came to him and begged him to rule over them against God's will, for no king had been anointed for that office. But Gideon had a righteous heart and said, "I will not rule over you, neither will my son rule over you: the Lord shall rule over you." At this Gideon had made one of the most difficult choices any man could make. He walked away from an offer to rule a nation. It is an unusual man who can refuse an offer for great power. Godly Gideon did the right thing. Then comes the seemingly small error. Gideon asked for the earrings from the Midianites (verse 24) and received a large supply of gold jewelry. He then formed that gold into a priestly ephod, a garment strictly reserved for the Levitical priesthood. This was not a proper action for Gideon. It crossed the line between the civil authority and the ecclesiastical authority. Gideon was outside his proper sphere of operation. And yet it seemed so right, to honor the God of Israel with the making of a golden ephod. The Lord would rule over them and this gold ephod was made to honor the Lord of their country. Everyone had contributed to make this magnificent gift to lift up the God of Israel. Perhaps, not so predictably, everything went wrong. The people did not raise their eyes to God when they saw the ephod. Instead our text informs us, "and all Israel went thither a whoring after it: which thing became a snare unto Gideon, and to his house."

Gideon thought he was doing the good and right thing by honoring God with an expensive gift. The problem for him was that God desires obedience rather than sacrifice. To obey is better than to invent an alternative, even if that alternative is well intentioned and expensive. The result of his foolish decision was that Israel went

47

chasing after it, and it became a snare for Gideon and his house. The well intentioned gift became an idol. This is not unlike what the church has done by erecting Christian schools. God told the parents to teach their children. For whatever reason, the parents decided to build Christian schools instead. It just seems so right! We build shiny buildings and hire fine Christian teachers to inspire our children. It keeps them out of the public institutions. What could be better? We think that God is pleased with our sacrifice, but He is not. God has already informed us of His will as regards education. He has instructed parents to teach their children. Christian schools are a golden ephod. They are built to honor God while disobeying His revealed will. The end of the matter will be that they will become a snare for us and our households. Christian parents need to stop whoring after this golden ephod and turn to obey their God.

## EXCEPTIONS TO THE RULE

I have been asked, "what about single parents who need to work, or parents that are incompetent to teach their children: How will their children be taught?" This is a valid concern, but it has to be treated as the exception, not the rule. Normal Christian behavior has to be directed by the clear teaching of Scripture. The odd or special situation may require families and churches to stretch beyond the ordinary. Our experience has been that there are many Christian homeschooling families that are happy to help their neighbors. The church may need to assist with a special program, etc. In the case of a widow with children, the church may need to help support her, so that she may stay at home to teach her children. The Bible instructs the church to help widows and orphans, so there is no conflict here. Perhaps the church just needs to take up the mantle given it by God. When the church obeys in one area it becomes easier to obey in another.

It may be useful to be reminded that parents teaching their own children has been the usual practice for most of history. The public school system as we know it is only about one hundred seventy years old. Five hundred years ago John Calvin wrote, "If a father of a family, in educating, governing, and managing his children…,"[1] thus discussing home education as the norm of his day. Surely if parents living in Reformation-era Europe could manage to teach their children we can have no excuse sufficient to pardon our neglect. We just need to start obeying. One of the best decisions my wife and I ever made was to teach our own children. It would be your best choice as well.

# CHAPTER 4

# To Socialize Our Children Properly

---

How Blessed is the man who does not
Walk in the counsel of the wicked,
Nor stand in the path of sinners,
*Nor sit in the seat of scoffers*

**Psalm 1:1**

The objection to homeschooling most often put forth by Christian parents is that their children will not be properly socialized. There is a great deal of superstition about this. It is almost as if, by having said the word socialization out loud, the discussion should be over. The culture so supports this argument that it is thought of by many parents as the final word. Supposedly, everyone knows there is virtually no way that a child could be socialized correctly outside of a typical school setting. Here we will take a Biblical and historical look at the idea and process of socialization.

Let us start with the word itself. The reader should understand that the concept and practice of socializing anyone is new historically. Two hundred years ago no one in America ever talked about socializing their children. The word did not exist.

It was Augusta Compte that introduced the study of sociology to the world. Mr. Compte hated Christian civilization and wanted to undermine and destroy it any way he could. The following quote from a sociology textbook will shed some light for us:

> To the great question of the Enlightenment—'What shall be put in place of the old traditional order?'—Compte replied, 'The scientific study of society and group life,' by which he meant impartial, unbiased observation.[1]

The "old traditional order" being discussed was the old Christian order, meaning Christian society. In Compte's time (mid-1800's) western civilization was quite Christian. Many of the concepts that underlayed all areas of life were based on Biblical principle. For those who hated that culture it was a difficult thing to know how to destroy it. Compte figured that an attack on the structure of the family and society might be highly effective. This is why he invented sociology. Sociology was presented as a scientific discipline that would reveal a more certain truth about family relationships than the Bible could. It was a way to circumvent the Scriptural principles for family relationships. Compte understood that sociology was never a science. In fact it was impossible for it to be (for details and documentation on this topic see my book *Advancing the Kingdom*). However, it provided an effective philosophical platform from which to attack Christian civilization. Compte's "scientific" word of truth was designed to replace God's revealed Word of truth.

When the topic of socialization comes up it is used with a variety of meanings. The word substitutes for a collection of worries carried by many non-homeschooling parents. Some of the surface concerns bear a little validity but the deeper root is one of sin. In many cases the word socialize obscures a deeper heart of rebellion.

Sometimes when people ask, how will my child be socialized?, they are wondering about issues of shyness. It is a genuine thought that their child will be too disconnected from the social world to speak with other people; kind of like having grown up in a closet and not ever meeting outsiders until suddenly being pushed out into the adult world at age twenty. They perhaps imagine a young woman of marriageable age having grown up in a soddy on the Kansas prairie, being tossed into Boston society. Why, she would not even know how to act around sophisticated bachelors her own age! They may take advantage of her innocence. It would be unfair and unwise to place her at such a disadvantage.

These images of naiveté, shyness, and social incompetence have only small merit. Admittedly there are some home educated students that are reared in such a way that they do not interact with the larger society enough. When they leave home they require some time to learn how to act and react properly in the world around them. However, most Christian homeschooled children are sheltered from the world but not disconnected from society. They participate with both adults and peers in social activities centered around church and family. They learn their social skills from mature Christian adults. Their parents are their primary models and tutors. The people they see at weekly church activities are a secondary source for social modeling, morality, attitudes, and behavior. The Bible is their moral code book, filling their hearts with virtuous stories and examples of holiness that they may imitate. All of this leads to a well formed character. It builds a sociable person ready to enter the adult arena with a superior moral conscience, and the graces of a lovely Christian spirit.

We also have to understand that students educated in schools often develop all sorts of social problems due to their having been in the school itself. When regular school kids demonstrate weird or anti-social tendencies hardly anyone accuses the school for that messed up child's behavior. Since school is normal the unsociable behavior exhibited by its students is also considered normal. No one attacks the schools for creating misfits. Yet for some reason if a home educated student displays a bit of unsociable behavior it is immediately assumed that homeschooling did it to him, and it is therefore an inferior teaching arrangement. Homeschooling will never turn out perfect people but neither will any other system. The government schools often graduate criminals (really unsocial people) from among their ranks, something that has not been a problem for Christian, home educated students.

## DEFINING SOCIALIZATION

Checking Webster's 1828 Dictionary will verify that the words socialize and socialization were not yet in use at that date. The fact that the words did not exist is instructive. It gives us clues as to how people thought about the development of their children. We can certainly determine that there was no mind-set anything like the modern thinking on this subject. When the word sociable was used it meant, "ready or disposed to unite in a general interest."[2] To be sociable meant that you would associate with someone. That is very much different than what is meant when people talk about the need to socialize children today.

According to the 1983 *American Heritage Dictionary* the word socialize means:

1. To place under public ownership or control.
2. To convert or adapt to social needs
3. To take part in social activities[3]

I will argue that all three of these definitions may be accurately used to describe the socialization occurring in American schools today, especially in the public schools. I will also argue that the whole concept of socialization is unbiblical at its root. The ideas of placing under public ownership and converting or adapting to social needs are particularly onerous.

# PUBLIC OWNERSHIP AND CONTROL

Anyone that has worked to understand Christian worldview issues will find their attention electrified at the dictionary definitions above. The contrasts with Biblical thought provoke alarm. The word socialize, and its attendant definitions, capture our interest because they so succinctly portray the nature of our present American society, particularly as applied to children.

When children are socialized, they are, by definition, being placed under "public ownership or control." The inception of that government ownership and control typically originates when the soon to be married couple obtains a marriage license. This license, once used only to license marriages for slaves, is now the unquestioned norm for all citizens including Christians. A marriage license makes the civil government a contractual party to the marriage and a holder of legal rights over the fruit of the marriage—namely the children. Therefore, in most cases, Christian families are begun with the civil authority having a strong measure of legal sway over their newly formed unions. There are many serious implications to this, but what we are focusing on in this context is the blitheness with which Christian parents subsume their God given office to civil authority. This practice opens a window for us into the mind of the twenty-first century Christian in America. It demonstrates how uncritical is our thinking and our acceptance of intrusion by civil government. We accept socialist legal control without a yawn, and we would never get stinky over such an accepted practice. We do not want to be found in contest over anything that is normal, for the approbation of public antipathy is too much to bear. After all, it is only a minor compromise.

Having entered the relationship with their government under these terms, it is only natural to present the child for official instruction at age five. Dutifully, mom and dad bring their little charges to preschool or kindergarten at the officially sanctioned government location. Here, the child is duly registered for a thirteen year stint

55

under the watchful eye of the local authorities. Of course Johnny or Suzie may occasionally receive permission for a short absence. Yet, everyone knows who is in charge, it is the party giving permission. Coercive, compulsory attendance laws keep the sheep corralled under government programs. Parents may bear them away for a short vacation, but the return of the children is fully expected. Public ownership has then been established. Even if public education were to allow more study at home, the education leaders will continue to pursue the same goals: thus the letter received by Charlotte Iserbyt from the Director of the office of Libraries and Learning Technology, U.S. Department of Education stating,

> In the future all education will take place in the home, using computer-assisted-instruction, but…we will always have the school buildings for **"socialization purposes."** [Emphasis mine].[4]

Further evidence concerning the attitude of government authorities toward ownership of the children may be found in the rapidly growing movement to medically treat students without the knowledge of the parents. We have also seen repeated attacks on homeschool families by social service departments, trying to drag them back into the government school systems under threat of taking away their children. The Home School Legal Defense Association has been the saving defense for many of these families. The stories are available monthly in their publication. The popular use of the term "human resources" by school planners to refer to students should also give us pause. For exactly whom are they to be resources? Is this really the correct perception of the student, as a *resource*? I thought the school and its teachers were to be the resource *for the students*. This appears to be a more serious version of the old bait and switch.

All of this to say, that the government claim to ownership of our children is a present and growing problem. It is a direct attack on the Christian family. This is part of what it means to socialize our children, and helps explain why we should *not* be trying to socialize them. The Bible sets parents, not the civil authority, over the child.

The family teaching Biblical tenets is to be the socializing agent not the schools.

## CONVERTING TO SOCIAL NEEDS

The second definition from *The American Heritage Dictionary* tells us that to socialize is, "To convert or adapt to social needs." It is the unrelenting application of this philosophy in the public schools that has prompted California State Senator Teresa Hughes to state, "We live in a society where children going to school have become comparable to soldiers going off to war."[5]

It is this sense of warfare against their historic Christian faith that has continued to turn parents away from the schools and toward homeschooling. They do not want the faith they inculcate at home to be displaced by a different religion, serving different purposes, and a different god. They have begun to understand that the secularism of the public institutions represents a competing religion that will by its very nature convert their children to its tenets, just as a Christian church may convert its opponents by its teaching influence. Discussing the socializing influence of Humanism, Henry Nelson Wieman states,

> Religion, then, as the word is here used, will mean a ruling commitment practiced by a community of individuals to what they believe creates, sustains, saves, and transforms human existence toward the greatest good.[6]

Parents are beginning to catch on to what the secular humanists have been saying for years: that Secular Humanism is a religion that reaps converts just as surely as any other religion. Their children are being converted and adapted to the social needs of the enemies of the church, just as the definition of socialization predicts. The avowed secularism of the government schools assures us that Christian thought is not to be dispensed within its walls. A Christian teacher may display some aspects of Biblical morality, but that teacher may never discuss any content of his/her faith. It is forbidden to teach such heresy in the temple of another religion. It is interesting to note Wieman's use of the word *saves* in the above quote. The use of that word is no happenstance. The anti-Christian mindset views the conversion of Christians from their faith to Humanism as an act of salvation, just as surely as a Christian evangelist does the turning of the lost to Christ.

Paul Kurtz, in his Preface to the *Humanist Manifestos I & II* informs us, "Humanism is a philosophical, religious, and moral point of view" and that it can be "as the expression of a quest for values and goals that we can work for and that can help us to take new directions."[7] His statement succinctly warns Christians as to exactly why they must avoid having their children socialized in the schools. The philosophy (religion by their own accounts) that rules the institutions is "an expression of a quest for values" that is being used to push the students toward a social order directly opposed to Biblical civilization. Thus, the socialization taking place will turn the hearts of the children away from their parents and Biblical faith.

In the chapter on worldview training, I laid the philosophical and theological foundations for building a Christian worldview and discussed how deeply that thinking should, but rarely does, affect the Christian curriculum. However, it is useful to note here that the Christian schools by their very nature are also working against the Biblical model of education. The Scriptures instruct parents to teach their children. The Christian school removes them from that home environment and socializes them into acceptance of group training, group thinking, and peer group associations that undermine the authority of parents. Students naturally view their teachers at school as having greater authority than their parents. After all, why would the parent send the child to be trained under these teachers, if the teachers did not have more authority and wisdom than the parents? The logic is inexorable. If the parents are the correct teachers, but the student is sent to someone else, there has to be a reason. That reasoning has both pragmatic and moral implications. The student senses all of this at some level, although he may not be able to express it with clarity. At any rate, the role of the parents is undercut when the child is institutionalized, even if in a Christian school.

## THE CONDITION OF THE HEART

So far all of this discussion about socializing children has been addressing parents that are perhaps ignorant of the pertinent considerations. It assumes that the parental motivations in bringing up the socialization question are honest, and that information is a direct help. For those parents I pray that I have made some helpful contribution.

The larger issue, though, is the condition of the heart for many parents. Often when the question is asked, "how will my child be socialized?" it is an attempt to escape from the social rejection the parent knows will come when the decision to homeschool is announced.

This issue of the condition of the heart is the deeper matter. St. Luke writes for us in the sixth chapter of his gospel, starting at the forty-third verse through verse forty-six saying:

> For a good tree bringeth not forth corrupt fruit; neither doth a corrupt tree bring forth good fruit. For every tree is known by its own fruit. For of thorns men do not gather figs, nor of a bramble bush gather they grapes. A good man out of the good treasure of his heart bringeth forth that which is good; and the evil man out of the evil treasure of his heart bringeth forth that which is evil: for of the abundance of the heart his mouth speaketh. And why do ye call me Lord, Lord, and do not the things which I say?

Here, Jesus teaches us that it is the heart that drives the will. The will does not drive the heart. Deep within each of us lie conditions and motivations deeper than the will. The Greek thought patterns that have been thoroughly built into our society over many centuries make us believe that cognitive choosing comes first, and the heart follows after. In this discourse Jesus teaches the opposite. "A good man out of the good treasure of his heart bringeth forth that which is good." The good treasure in the heart precedes the good deeds. Jesus warns, "for of the abundance of the heart his mouth speaketh."

It is precisely at this point where the word of God and the question, "How will my children be socialized?" meet. The question is often not sincere. It is, rather, a covering over for the parent's lack of an obedient heart. God's commands for parents to teach their children are strong and clear. What is lacking is a heart that is right with the Lord.

A parent choosing to home educate will almost certainly be challenged by family and friends on the decision. There will be accusations that the parents are irresponsible, that the children will be isolated, that they need help from professionals, that the children will lose valuable relationships, that it is not healthy for parents to teach their own children, along with endless objections, much of it designed to discourage the parents from their appointed duties. All of this brings fear to the hearts of parents. The fear of man over rides the fear of God. This is the sin. Sin is when we fear the wrong party.

## Whom Do We Fear?

Job wrote, "And unto man he said, Behold, the fear of the Lord, that is wisdom; and to depart from evil is understanding" (Job 28:28). We are faced with this choice as we consider obedience to God's call to teach our children. Will we fear God and depart from evil? For too many parents the answer is hidden behind false questions about the socialization of their children. Meanwhile Jesus continues to ask, "And why do you call me Lord, Lord, and do not the things which I say?" The reason is that they are not entirely sure that Jesus is Lord. They call Him Lord but will not obey. More facts will not help. It is a struggle of the heart.

I think every man and woman on the planet has a fear of being weird. If they want to avoid being weird the only way to do it is to fit in with the group in which they run. The Christian that is committed to obedience to God cannot choose to fit in with a godless peer group. That leaves just two basic choices; they may be rejected by their friends or they may spend their time in a friendlier group. Maybe, sometimes, they can do a little of both. The problem with remaining in a situation where they are always rejected is that they just get worn down. So there is great value in being in community with like minded people. My wife and I moved to our present location largely to be near a church full of believers who think as we think and live as we live. We are not spiritual giants, so we maintain fellowship with those who are, or at least are trying to be. The fruit from this situation is that we spend a lot less energy fighting useless battles. We can concentrate on accomplishing worthwhile work for the Kingdom. Living in a community of like-minded believers is very freeing. We can mutually encourage each other to live what we say we believe. I recommend it highly. Move if you have to. If Lot had understood this, his wife never would have been turned to salt—think about it.

## OVERCOMING THE WORLD

Scripture reminds us:

> For this is the love of God, that we keep his commandments: **and his commandments are not grievous**. For whatsoever is born of God overcometh the world: and this is the victory that overcometh the world, even our faith. Who is he that overcometh the world, but he that believeth that Jesus is the Son of God? [Emphasis mine].

**1 John 5:3–5**

This talk about overcoming the world can be highly convicting. The God we serve expects His people to be overcomers which means acting as necessary to do God's will. It speaks of engaging in battle. The text tells us the commandments are not grievous. That is curious because often they are treated as being grievous, especially when we are talking about home educating our children. It is as if we are being asked to do something monstrous. Actually, the blessing is all ours if we will take it. It is a privilege to teach our children, not a burden. Those who see it as grievous are not viewing the family through Godly eyes.

We are supposed to be overcoming the world, if we are born of God. Keeping the commandments is the evidence that we are born of God. Our faith gives us the victory that overcomes the world and keeps His commandments. All of these things operate together; faith, victory, overcoming the world, and keeping the commandments of God. Our faith and lives are to be seamless. We believe and we obey. True faith brings conformance with God's will, and conformance is a display of true faith.

Disobedience, therefore, is often a sign of a lack of faith. That is why John brings the statement, "Who is he that overcometh the world, but he that believeth that Jesus is the Son of God?" True faith does overcome the world. Given this knowledge we can safely say that when we see irresolute disobedience to clear Biblical commands, the problem is likely that the individual lacks a belief that Jesus is the Son of God. In other words, they do not have saving faith. They may be very religious and attend all manner of church functions, but if they refuse to obey the known will of God then their true salvation is in question. We cannot know for certain the status of another man's salvation but we can see the fruit on the tree, so to speak. Sometimes a steadfast refusal to educate children according to Biblical principle is an indication of a lack of knowledge but it may also be the fruit of an unregenerate spirit. We should not be quick to judge, but neither should we expect the dead to act like the living.

Opponents to homeschooling often bring up the questions about socialization, but almost never are able to describe any real content behind what they are asking. If we say "What do you mean by socialization?" they cannot explain what they mean. The parents want to fit into society, and there is an understanding that their families will never fit in once they embrace homeschooling. *Socialization* is the word that sums their fears.

Socialization is an idea in direct opposition to Biblical thought. This is why we should not seek the socialization of our children. Socialized children will likely spend their lives working against the Kingdom of God just as a matter of natural habit. They will have been taught to do so under the socializing influence of a humanist mindset, taught by example, and assumed in every classroom at the government institutions. We must keep them away from these socializing forces and rear them in Biblical righteousness. That is the alternative.

# CHAPTER 5

# Righteousness is the Goal

---

Blessed are they which do hunger
And thirst after righteousness: for
They shall be filled.

**Matthew 5:6**

In the last chapter we saw that the goal of the schools, oftentimes, is to socialize the children. We have rejected that goal as unbiblical and immoral. What, then, is the proper goal for Christian instruction? What are we supposed to be trying to accomplish? What does God say is the correct content or direction for our teaching? Those are some of the questions I will try to answer in this chapter. I will enunciate some specifics, and derive meaning from, the many texts that directly discuss Godly instruction.

When the Bible addresses teaching and instruction it approaches the topic from a decidedly different perspective than today's society, and particularly today's educational establishment. Virtually all non-Christian educators believe that man is essentially good. They view him as being damaged by his environment, but good at his heart. Having assumed this innate goodness, the humanist educator believes that the only need is to fill the student's mind with correct information. Therefore, education is a matter of imparting data. Given enough facts the students are expected to arrive at logical and moral conclusions. Their lives are to be built on a sturdy foundation of information. Knowledge will be their source for the planning of their lives.

This standard is, in theory, the philosophical team of oxen that turns the wheels of the educational machinery. Of course anyone that has looked with any care at the actual works and products of the present (especially government) school systems, knows that the pursuit of knowledge has long been abandoned. It is a dream or a memory, but has no attachment to what is actually going on in these edifices. So even the fallacious notion of knowledge being the salvation of man is really just that, a notion, long buried, whose meaning has become insensible to those who try to keep the gears turning (or even just lurching and grinding).

## THE FEAR OF THE LORD

Knowledge will not save us. The fear of the Lord will save us. This is why Solomon warns "The fear of the Lord is the beginning of knowledge" (Proverbs 1:7). There is no value in trying to discover knowledge without first having a healthy fear of the God who invented the world of knowledge. Without proper fear we do not carry the correct attitude to approach the universe or the university.

Evangelicals often interpret Scripture that refers to the fear of God as being hyperbole; as if God does not really mean fear He just means great respect or a worshipful attitude. After all, He has told us we are His friends (John 15:15). Why would He expect us to fear Him? The answer is that even though God is our friend, He is also our mighty Creator. A fear of His displeasure is a healthy thing. It keeps us from unsanctified behavior. His justice is fearful, but His blessings are to be sought. God wants to bless us. So the pursuit of knowledge ought always to begin with the fear of God.

Our pilgrim forefathers gave us a good example as people that feared God and made the right decisions. They valued the things that God values. William Bradford records their difficult lives in Holland before they came to this continent, "…they fell to such trades and employments as they best could, valuing their peace and spiritual comfort above any other riches whatsoever."[1] They valued their peace and spiritual comforts more than any riches whatsoever. That describes a pursuit of righteousness that should inspire us to action. Our difficulties are not the same, and in fact they are certainly less. Yet the need to hunger and thirst after righteousness is paramount for Christians in every age. The battle we face is for the teaching of our children. Do we fear God sufficiently to value their proper instruction over other comforts? Will we be righteous or will we be cowards? Whom or what do we fear?

## DEFINING RIGHTEOUSNESS

The fear of God is also the beginning of righteousness (Proverbs 2:5–13). We cannot learn true righteousness without first learning to fear the God who declares what is righteous. God is the definer of righteousness. It is His law that informs the mind and the heart. Righteousness belongs first to God. We learn righteousness from Him. Therefore, Paul's maxim to Timothy (1 Timothy 1:5), "But the goal of our instruction is love from a pure heart and a good conscience and a sincere faith" distills for us the spirit needed to imbibe the best beginnings for a Christian curriculum. Righteousness is the goal of Biblically based instruction.

### Love From A Pure Heart

The quote from First Timothy carries three parts, the first being: love from a pure heart. This would be as opposed to love or hatred from a wicked heart. As I mentioned before, the condition of the heart is at the bottom of everything. It is the heart that determines what our will may choose. An impure heart cannot push forward righteousness. It may imitate a righteous condition, but the root is always dead from beginning to end. Its mimicry of purity only hides the impure, which must show itself eventually. A pure heart is a gift from the Holy Spirit to the redeemed. There is no other source of purity. The very meaning of the word pure is subsumed under the word holy in Holy Spirit. Purity is a component of holiness.

Love from the pure and holy heart is the first goal of our instruction. This fact collides rudely with the goals for instruction found in the school systems in America. Since the government schools run on the notion that morality is relative, it is impossible for them to define terms like pure or holy. They cannot. By their nature these concepts fall outside the circles of investigation believed proper for public discussion. Words with strong moral connotation are by necessity bypassed for weaker adjectives like feel, loving, or diverse. Stronger descriptive words such as homophobe or greedy are reserved for those opposed to the mucky, moral milieu upon which the educational institutions are constructing their futures. The amoral nomenclature of the schools is averse to that of the church. None of this bodes good will for those seeking sturdy moral strictures to underpin their lives. A pure heart will have to be developed somewhere else.

The word love is thrown up and down by everyone. Its meaning however, is rarely defined. Our Bible calls for "love from a pure heart." So the source of love must be morally pure. Biblical morality sustains love as a matter of definition. Love as the world describes it is no love at all, since it is based outside of God, who is the source of love. God is love. Without Him, love is an emotion derived from the self, which is always focused inward. This is why Jesus told us to love our neighbor as ourselves. He knew that we always consider ourselves first, due to our fallen natures. This natural love for ourselves can only be remade through the power and love of Christ. Therefore the love found in the world is rooted in unclean hearts and can never be what Christian love is. Worldly love is an imitator that serves itself in the end. Consequently, "love from a pure heart" will never derive from a school system established and operated in direct violation of God's revealed will. "The goal of our instruction is love from a pure heart…" There is no good future in these non-Biblical systems for Christian students.

## A Good Conscience

The second condition needed to produce love is a "good conscience." Since the goal of Christian instruction is "love from a pure heart and a good conscience…" we have to believe that it is imperative for our children to go through life with a good conscience. The conscience differs from the heart in that the conscience responds to what the person does. The heart underlies and drives all that we do. The conscience informs us as to the morality of what we have done (Romans 2:15). The conscience testifies to the fact that the law is written on our hearts. It seems to work with our emotions, which explains why we feel guilty after having wronged someone.

A good conscience requires a good life. That is, a life free from sin, particularly known or repeated sin. I do not mean to say that any of us will live sinless. Certainly every man sins daily; thus the need for continuing repentance. However, for the Christian sanctification is to be a normal, continuing process. We are conquerors in Christ as we advance against the powers and temptations set against us. The unsaved have no such privilege. Their conscience accuses them of their unlawful behavior daily, yet they refuse to repent. The unredeemed cannot have a good conscience due to the continuing presence of unforgiven sin.

Our question as Christian parents is, How may a student maintain a good conscience while promiscuously tramping among the thorns sown for their destruction? Every day their "righteous souls are vexed" just as was Lot while in Sodom. The amoral or typically immoral environment in the schools will vex a righteous heart. The filthy language in the hallways alone is sufficient to drive away a sincere Christian. Our children and others have often confirmed the coarseness of the talk encountered while making only a short walk through the local institutions. This is not a scientific test, but it is a heart test that confirms the fact that these institutions are not places for students that wish to maintain a pure heart and good conscience. The morality of the Christian student will be under attack daily from every direction. Immoral sexual pressure and the common breaking of every commandment will surround them as a matter of course. Yet our God has told us that a good conscience is required if we are to have love as the result of our instruction. Remember, the goal is "love from … a good conscience." If this is the goal, how will it be advanced if the student's conscience is continually burdened with true guilt built up from constant temptation, and the nearly inevitable yielding to it?

A good conscience is obtained by living separate from sinful, destructive influences. Separate does not mean to never encounter, but it does mean that our children are not required to swim in a sewer. God has assigned the home as the place for child rearing and instruction. Parents that obey this model will likely rear children that really do have good consciences and the loving hearts that follow. This is a worthy goal.

## Sincere Faith

Paul mentions "…a sincere faith" as the third element supporting love as the goal of our instruction. If we rear children that have the pure heart and good conscience he discusses, we may hold a realistic expectation that our children will maintain a sincere faith. This is the prize so many parents see slip away as their children near adulthood. After years of having their faith assaulted in an anti-Christian school environment, children of Christian parents often display a faith that is not sincere. The insincerity displays itself as a lack of interest in spiritual things, no reading of God's word, inappropriate dress, disrespect for parents, unregenerate close friends, failure to tithe, and no interest in kingdom building work. All of these things flow from a life that was never inspired to live in a love relationship with their Creator.

If "the goal of our instruction is love…from a sincere faith," we cannot fulfill this Godly goal by acting and living like the world in the area of education. The temptation is so very great to just be comfortable in rearing our children. We do not want to be at war with the culture or our families. It is so enticing to believe we can disobey God and somehow fill in the gaps on weekends or in the evenings. Yet disobedience does not bear good fruit. We know this, but still there is a hope that we can escape the destructiveness of sin, while shrugging our shoulders and pushing off the responsibility for another day. Our disobedient Christian friends make it easy to slouch along to Gomorrah, to use a phrase from Robert Bork. The familiarity of sin breeds contempt for righteousness. That contempt is at the root of an insincere faith in both the parents and their children. We cannot expect our children to have a sincere faith when the parents lack that same quality. The choice is before us to obey or disobey. What is the goal of our instruction?

## Solomon on Righteousness

At the beginning of this chapter I used the heading to summarize the Apostle Paul's instruction to Timothy by saying—*The Goal is Righteousness*. To propose that the goal of our instruction should be righteousness is an idea immediately hostile to the tenets of the present education establishment. The appearance is, that they are unsure what their goal might be. To impart knowledge may be a part of it. However, as I will demonstrate in a later chapter, the pursuit of knowledge is minimal by any objective standard.

When we consider that neither righteousness nor knowledge are the goals of their instruction it becomes increasingly difficult to pin down exactly why we would want our children in the government or private schools. What is it that we are expecting to be imparted in these places? Home taught children are regularly out-performing their schooled peers in both quality of character issues, and in all measurable knowledge accumulation as well. But I do not want to get too far afield from the point of this chapter.

When we understand that the first and proper goal of our instruction is righteousness we are announcing a direction unfamiliar within our American society. It is also unfamiliar within the church. The idea that the mastery of knowledge is to be the heart of all education permeates our thinking. In a later chapter I will discuss the importance of acquiring a wide knowledge. However, the Bible elevates the building of a righteous life above that of just learning facts. We need both, but moral development and wisdom are of first importance. This is why we are going to take a deeper look at the beginning of the book of Proverbs.

The book of Proverbs begins this way:

> The proverbs of Solomon the son of David, king of Israel; to know wisdom and instruction; to perceive the words of understanding; to receive the instruction of wisdom, justice, and judgment, and equity; to give subtilty to the simple, to the young man knowledge and discretion. A wise man will hear, and will increase learning; and a man of understanding shall attain unto wise counsels: to understand a proverb, and the interpretation; the words of the wise, and their dark sayings. The fear of the Lord is the beginning of knowledge: but fools despise wisdom and instruction. My son hear the instruction of thy father, and forsake not the law of thy mother…

When the apostle Paul taught that "The goal of our instruction is love out of a pure heart…" etc., he was summarizing the Old Testament doctrine on this subject, particularly the early chapters of Proverbs. These first verses of Proverbs are written specifically to let us know the purpose of the book. It is "to receive the instruction of wisdom, justice, and judgment, and equity…" These four areas of study were given as the foundation for a proper education. None of these would make any list coming out of the present education establishment. The Biblical ideals are at cross purposes with those of the educational elite.

These four areas of study were Solomon's core curriculum. As we look through the Proverbs we find many of them addressed to each of the specific categories he mentions. All of these have to do with living a righteous life—being a righteous person. Solomon mentions nothing about history, sociology, mathematics, or language skills. He does not push Latin, Greek, or romantic writings. None of these are on his list and yet Solomon is still recognized as the world's wisest man.

The first subject Solomon names is wisdom. The other categories are much more specific. Wisdom is general in that it consists of principles that may be applied to a variety of circumstances in life. Wisdom tells us how to live rightly within the, sometimes confounding, circumstances of this life. Most of the Proverbs fall under this broad heading.

The value of wisdom is explained in the third chapter starting at verse thirteen, "Happy is the man that findeth wisdom," through thirty-five "The wise shall inherit glory." Solomon lets us know that all of the things we value most in life are to be gained through application of wisdom. This is not to say that we may ever overthrow God's sovereign will. His plans stand above all of our striving. However, it is also true that a wisely lived life will be marked by the blessings Solomon mentions, i.e. chapter three, verses:

[16]Length of days is in her right hand and in her left hand riches and honour.

[17]All her paths are peace.

[18]She [wisdom] is a tree of life…happy is everyone that retaineth her.

[23]Thou shalt walk in thy way safely

<sup>24</sup>When thou liest down, thou shalt not be afraid: yea, thou shalt lie down, and thy sleep shall be sweet.

<sup>26</sup>For the Lord shall be thy confidence, and shall keep thy foot from being taken.

<sup>35</sup>The wise shall inherit glory: but shame shall be the promotion of fools.

These are significant promises. They fill in for much of what is normally hoped for by parents from a school or knowledge based education. When everything is considered to its end, are these not the things that matter the most? We want to walk through life safely, be financially prosperous, be protected from the snares of life (He "shall keep thy foot from being taken"), be at peace, and our sleep to be sweet.

None of these blessings are promised, in Scripture, to those who finish a school program. They are promised to those who find wisdom—paths of living and acting that direct us in a righteous life. Perhaps we are worried that if we do not live like the world lives, and do what the world does, in respect to schooling, that we will end up being ashamed of the way our lives turn out. We are worried that we will end up being shown to be fools. Yet the writer of Psalm 119 gives us a better hope about these things saying, (verse six) "Then shall I not be ashamed, when I have respect unto all thy commandments." When we teach first the wisdom and commandments of God, our children will not have to be ashamed. It is God's faithful promise. The necessity is for us to rediscover the mindset and lifestyle that promote this Biblically based approach. We need to break from the culturally mandated norms for education and return to the Creator's. It is a different view of life and of what is important. Morality and principle come first, and other knowledge comes second. It is a matter of priority.

As a practical matter my wife and I found that by concentrating on rearing wise, obedient children we ended up with a family situation that was much more conductive to teaching other knowledge.

We were able to communicate all types of teaching more easily due to the children's attitudes toward learning being more embracing and respectful. The willful or unwise child will often rebel at having to study anything good. Therefore a lack of wisdom leads to a lack of knowledge.

Solomon warns us in Proverbs 4:23, "Keep thy heart with all diligence; for out of it are the issues of life." It is the condition of the heart that sets the course for life, not what degrees we earn. School degrees can be useful, but a wise and righteous heart is more so. This is why education should concentrate on these issues first.

The early chapters of Proverbs are filled with warnings against sexual impurity. Some of the most important wisdom Solomon had to give circled around this issue, and who would know better? The man with hundreds of wives and concubines found out through experience what God had said all along. Now, we live in a time when sexual morality is in desperate need of being revived. Parents may do this in the home. The schools will teach all manner of folly, directing the students to destroy (sometimes literally) themselves, for the sake of temporary pleasure. The schools will undermine good instruction in this area. This is no small thing. Solomon put it near the top of the list.

## UNDERSTANDING JUSTICE

The second of Solomon's four stated teaching purposes in Proverbs (1:3) is to instruct in justice. Once again, this choice is not one most of us would think important as a school subject. We think of justice as something left to the courts and attorneys. Why would justice be near the top of Solomon's list?

The reasoning behind this priority of learning justice has to do with the understanding that God's law is the ultimate rule for both individual behavior and the courts. There is no separation in terms of the behavior required. This is why so many Scriptures connect justice and judgment to personal morality and action. Solomon reminds us in Proverbs 21:3 that, "To do justice and judgment is more acceptable to the Lord than sacrifice." The prophet Isaiah instructs (Isaiah 56:1) "Thus saith the Lord, keep ye judgment, and do justice: for my salvation is near to come, and my righteousness to be revealed." Psalm 98:8–9 reminds us, "…let the hills be joyful together before the Lord; for he cometh to judge the earth: with righteousness shall he judge the world, and the people with equity."

When Solomon says that he is writing Proverbs to instruct in "wisdom, justice, and judgment, and equity" (Proverbs 1:3) there are really only two major categories of training here: the first being wisdom, and the second, justice. Judgment and equity are concepts that work along with justice. They flesh out some of the larger meaning.

The broader message then, is that the work of the parents is to train their children to think and act justly according to God's law. The prophet Micah teaches this same concept in his beautiful verse "He hath showed thee, O man, what is good; and what doth the Lord require of thee, but to do justly, and to love mercy, and to walk humbly with thy God" (Micah 6:8). Much of the Christian life is summarized around the concept of justice and living justly. This induces us to understand that Christian parents must both know and teach God's law to their children. It is impossible to think that children will come to understand justice if they do not know and reasonably understand the law of God. Man's law is often unjust or even immoral. God's law is perfect as the Psalmist declares (Psalm 19:7). I cannot delve into a detailed discussion of the law here; abler men have already done so and their books are available.[2] Suffice it to say that most Christian parents have given almost no thought to the importance of teaching God's law to their children. Solomon considered it to be of high importance, but the modern church and Christian parents usually do not.

By teaching children at home we have a tremendous opportunity to impart this critical knowledge. The schools certainly will not do this work. Many of the most fruitful discussions I had with my children were centered around Biblical law. By understanding God's law with some clarity, they were able to develop righteous convictions concerning personal morality. Righteousness is the goal of our instruction; therefore the teaching of God's law becomes paramount.

The surrounding culture places every parent under unrelenting pressure to conform to its standards. While homeschooling is a growing practice, still, the message of society is that you are a little bit quacky if you try it yourself. Trying to conform home teaching to Biblical standards adds another hurdle for the culture resisting Christian parent. Yet God is faithful. His concern is that we rear righteous seed, ready to take dominion in the earth as He gives opportunity. We cannot succeed if we fail to teach the core lessons of wisdom, morality and justice. The other subject matter will follow. Our students will be both righteous and well learned. Teaching our children to live righteous lives is to be the goal of our instruction. From this base of righteous moral conviction, they should advance to a mastery of other curriculum.

## CHAPTER 6

# To Advance Covenant Faithfulness

---

Yet he hath made with me an everlasting
covenant, ordered in all things, and sure

**2 Samuel 23:5**

The concept of the covenant in Scripture always involves a generational view. To think generationally necessarily means that education has to be considered. Education is like a fluid that flows across time. It may either cleanse or pollute depending on its content. Our understanding of God's covenants will have a direct effect on how we educate our children.

The basic idea of a covenant is the making of a promise. The Bible describes various types of covenants. They may be between two people such as mentioned by the prophet Malachi at chapter two, and verse fourteen, "...she is thy companion, and the wife of thy covenant;" thus defining the marriage agreement as a covenant arrangement. Both parties swear to it under the greater authorities of God and His church. In this covenant there are promises and conditions binding the parties, e.g. faithfulness being understood as paramount for the covenant to remain binding.

God's covenant with man is similar but differs in that God sets all of the terms and conditions and then swears upon Himself since there is no one greater by which to swear. The key covenant of this type is described in Genesis chapter fifteen. Here a customary cutting of covenant is described. God has Abram take a heifer, a goat, and a ram, divide them in half, and he laid "each piece one against the other" (verse 10). Then the text tells us, "And when it came to pass, that, when the sun went down, and it was dark, behold a smoking furnace, and a burning lamp that passed between those pieces. In the same day the Lord made a covenant with Abraham, saying, 'Unto thy seed have I given this land...'" (verses 17–18).

In this case the promise was made by God and sealed by Him alone as evidenced by God's symbolic presence of the smoking furnace and burning lamp passing between the pieces where Abraham did not pass through. This was God's work and covenant sealed with His own sign. So the covenant between God and man is one sided in this respect. God sets the terms and man responds. The covenant however, is with those who believe. Prior to this cutting of covenant Genesis tells us, "And he [Abraham] believed in the LORD; and he counted it to him for righteousness" (Genesis 15:6).

The covenant with Abraham and his seed was expanded by God as time passed. When Abraham was ninety-nine years old God promised him, "And I will establish my covenant between me and thee and thy seed after thee in their generations for an everlasting covenant, to be a God unto thee, and to thy seed after thee..." (Genesis 17:7). And God said unto Abraham, "Thou shalt keep my covenant therefore, thou, and thy seed after thee in their generations" (Genesis 17:9).

We can see another expansion of the covenant between God and His people in the twenty-eighth chapter of Deuteronomy. Here God promises blessings for the nation of Israel if they obey His law, and curses if they do not. The passage concludes in chapter twenty-nine, verse one, "These are the words of the covenant, which the Lord commanded Moses to make with the children of Israel...," that is, with His covenant people. The children of Israel were God's children by covenant, beginning with Abraham and continuing through his line of chosen people.

## MESSENGER OF THE COVENANT

All of God's people are His by covenant. This is why the Testaments are commonly referred to as the Old Covenant and the New Covenant. The prophet Malachi makes the bridge between the Old Covenant and the New Covenant in the third chapter, verse one, saying, "…and the Lord, whom ye seek, shall suddenly come to his temple, even the **messenger of the covenant**, whom ye delight in: behold he shall come, saith the LORD of hosts" [Emphasis mine]. The book of Hebrews tells us, "God, who at sundry times and in divers manners spake in time past unto the fathers by the prophets, hath in these last days spoken unto us by his Son…" (Hebrews 1:1–2). So this same Son whom we worship and serve is also the Messenger of the covenant. His message is covenantal. We must understand the import of this as we approach our educational duties. Everything we do is going to be in relation to the Messenger of the covenant. Consequently, in our imitation of Christ we are also to be messengers of the covenant. This is why it is imperative for home educators to understand covenant thought. We have to live out covenant principles, teaching them both by example and by spoken and written means. The messenger of the covenant must understand its precepts and live a life consonant with them. These are the duties of the messengers of the covenant.

Christ, as *the* messenger of the covenant declares, "This cup is the new testament [covenant] in my blood, which is shed for you" (Luke 22:20). The covenant is new primarily in that it is now sealed with the blood of Christ instead of being sealed with the blood of bulls and goats. The covenant itself was repeatedly declared to be everlasting (Genesis 17:7, Psalm 105:8, 2 Samuel 23:5, Hebrews

13:20). So the covenant is with those who, like Abraham, believe God and have it counted unto them for righteousness. In the New Testament era we have more information about how that salvation is effected but the way of salvation (and entry into the covenant) has never changed—we believe God and He counts it to us for righteousness. Our faith is both from God and in God. It is He who cuts covenant with us.

## COVENANT IS EVERLASTING

Since we are to live with God in a covenantal relationship we have to understand what this means. What are the terms and conditions of the covenant? How does homeschooling relate to a covenantal life-style?

Knowing that the covenant between God and His people is "an everlasting covenant" communicates to us the permanence of the arrangement. Covenantal living is to be a life-long pursuit for us. We do not simply take note that the Bible discusses the covenant and then move on to other things. Living under the covenant still affects us. There is a continuing call to live within its terms.

## BLESSING AND CURSING

Some of the most prominent aspects of the covenant are the promises of blessing for obedience to God and cursings for disobedience. These are particularly emphasized as applied to the nation. Deuteronomy communicates this in great detail in the twenty-eighth and twenty-ninth chapters. There we find a long list of promised blessings to the nation that serves the Lord and an even longer list of curses for a disobedient nation. I do not want to dwell on this particular aspect except to say that when a nation violates the covenant its people may expect to receive judgment from God. The application for us is very direct. When our nation violates God's commands to educate our children we are lining ourselves up for the curses God promises for the disobedient. And, we can certainly observe many curses on the nation, especially as related to the schools. Rampant immorality, high illiteracy rates, astoundingly ignorant graduates, and tremendous costs and taxes related to the system, to name a few. The immoral, ignorant students produced are a curse to the nation. As these foolish students take their places in society their lack of moral rectitude drags the nation to a diminishing moral and spiritual condition. Children should be a blessing not a curse. These reasons in themselves are sufficient to bring our children home. Christians should be producing a blessed generation that will attract to our nation the blessings of the One we worship.

As examples of God's blessing and cursing on the nations it is useful to look to some of the European nations (especially since leftist Americans adore everything European). For it was Germany, England, and France that were blessed with the great preachers and reformers of the reformation era—Luther from Germany, Calvin from France, and Tyndale from England. As these nations abandoned their God-given heritages, God gave them over to judgment. Thus the three destroyed each other twice in the last century, and all have been cursed with socialistic governments ever since. These are three nations that need to repent and regain the blessings of God. There are lessons for America in this. May we not miss them.

## A GENERATIONAL VIEW

A covenantal life style is one that views all of life through generational eyes. Modern American society is thoroughly egalitarian; meaning that the individual is normally at the center of every decision. It is the happiness, progress, and fulfillment of the individual (ourselves) to which we direct all of our energy. When it comes to future planning we Christians act like the dominant culture. Most of us do not give much thought to how the kingdom of God might be built up through those who come after us. We are not generational thinkers and we are not kingdom builders, at least not in any sense that reaches beyond our own lives. This helps to explain why the churches usually are not dismayed about the overwhelming loss of their children to the world. There is no generational vision so the loss of their children is acceptable in the general scheme of things. Often there is no remorse expressed even from the pulpit because the pastor's children are also lost, having rejected their parents' faith in their teenage years, if not before.

There is a marked contrast between the Biblical covenantal view and popular egalitarianism. Everywhere I look in the Scriptures God is found describing His relationship with His people in generational language. When God makes His covenant with Abraham He says, "Thou shalt keep my covenant therefore, thee and all thy seed after thee in their generations" (Genesis 17). Exodus 2:24 reinforces the generational perspective as the bondage of Israel in Egypt is discussed saying, "And God heard their groaning, and God remembered his covenant with Abraham, with Isaac, and with Jacob." These references and others too many to mention all communicate the same thing—that God covenants with generations of people not just individuals. In fact it is impossible to find any covenant statement from God that is not generational in its outlook. Therefore, if we are to think and live Biblically we have to approach life from that covenantal, generational approach.

Because of these things home education fulfills an irreplaceable role in the work of the family. By educating our children in the home we were able to build the relationships with, and respect from, our children that were needed to seal in their hearts the grand vision to build God's kingdom. Now they are committed to teach their children likewise. The mission has become generational. The people of the covenant carry forward the work of the kingdom through their children and their children's children. The kingdom of God is unstoppable, especially when built in this way.

A study of the family of the famous preacher Jonathan Edwards was made one hundred seventy-three years after his marriage. The study showed that his 1400 member extended family had produced:

- 13 college presidents
- 65 professors
- 56 physicians and a dean of a medical school
- 1 Vice President of the United States
- Ministers in platoons, with nearly 100 of them becoming missionaries overseas

Besides these there were a large number of honorable men, office holders in government, etc. All of this came from a single family line that began with a covenantal family view. The results roll through history doing damage to the Devil's plans for decades.

## RESULTS OF DISOBEDIENCE

As my wife and I worked through our homeschooling years we met a great deal more people that disagreed with the direction we had taken than those who supported it. Having been told that our children would not be socialized properly, or very often warned that we just had to get them into high school at least, we sometimes worried that maybe those well intended cluckings might hold some merit. Looking back we see a litter of Christian families that lost their children, several to a point of being drunkards and petty criminals, and regularly marrying outside the faith. These parents have cut off their own posterity. By shrinking before the disapprobation of the society they now have nothing to show from their child rearing years than children who will expend their lives in the pursuit of mammon. Their children live for a different faith and build a kingdom in opposition to that in which their parents believed. Not only have they lost a generation, they have actually reared children who attack God's kingdom everywhere they go. The responsibility for this lies first with the parents and secondarily with the churches that kept their silence while the children of the covenant were destroyed in the citadels of man—government schools. Having allowed their children to dwell in the camp of the enemy for thirteen years the parents now pray for the return of their children to a faith the parents disobeyed for so long. God does answer prayer but it is a miracle for which they are praying. The children are simply living out the values they were taught in the schools to which they were sent. The irreligious lives of the children should be the expected result of a humanistic education. The public is receiving that for which it pays.

The result of living a non-covenantal life is mentioned by the Apostle Paul. He states concerning this issue:

> Wherefore remember, that ye being in time past Gentiles in the flesh...That at that time ye were without Christ, being aliens from the commonwealth of Israel, and strangers from the covenants of promise, having no hope, and without God in the world

**Ephesians 2:11–12**

This passage is directed toward those outside the faith who entered the covenant through regeneration. Yet there are a couple of things we can note from these verses. One is that the covenants are "covenants of promise," indicating the promises of blessing in Scripture for those who live in obedience to the covenants of God. By obeying God we can expect His blessing on our lives. This does not mean all of life will be trouble free but it does mean that God is our friend and that He wills good for us. A difficult life lived in God's grace beats living as an enemy of God. Paul also talks of those who live outside the covenant as "having no hope." This lack of hope is what we see in parents that have reared their children without a covenantal expectation. The parents often believe that the loss of their children is just a part of living in a broken world. There is no sense of God working through their family for "a thousand generations" (Deuteronomy 7:9), which is a Biblical metaphor meaning a very long time. Under this view hopelessness is the norm and Christians just have to tough it out and wait for heaven. Once their children have turned against the faith and have left home it is almost impossible to figure out what can be done. No amount of pleading or arguing seems to work. Hopelessness is the inheritance for those who try to live outside the covenant.

**"The logical outcome of defensive warfare is defeat."**

**Napoleon Bonaparte**

Families that live averse to the covenant model in education are always on the defensive concerning good teaching. Their children bring home doctrines and ideas that are at war with the faith once given. The Biblical model is not defensive. It is offensive because it prepares the child spiritually to bring the battle to the enemies of the church. A well taught child leaves home not just able to defend his faith but to assert the crown rights of Jesus in the larger society. The Apostle Paul wrote,

> For the weapons of our warfare are not carnal, but mighty through God to the pulling down of strong holds; Casting down imaginations and every high thing that exalts itself against the knowledge of God…"

**2 Corinthians 10:4–5**

So pulling down strongholds is the proper work of the church. Parents are to prepare young men and women who will bring the battle to the army of darkness. Schools will not help us prepare our children but we can do so at home. We need to be planning to take back the culture not just defend the vestiges of a dying faith. Home education is a big key to that kind of success.

"All the paths of the Lord are mercy and truth unto such as keep his covenant and his testimonies," so says king David in Psalm 25: 10. We need His mercy and truth to begin this work of home education. When a husband and wife make the decision to act generationally in their approach to family life and education they are forced to rethink everything they have been taught. I believe God extends mercy and leads His people into truth as they pursue this righteous way. We begin by keeping covenant and His testimonies. He blesses by revealing further truth and showing mercy.

## A SEPARATE PEOPLE

There is another part to this process. David continues four verses later in the same Psalm, "The secret of the Lord is with them that fear him; and he will show them his covenant." The fear of the Lord is not just an emotion, but rather it includes a heart and will to do what He commands. As His people advance in their fear of God he shows them His covenant. We are continually discovering more about what it means to live covenantally with our God and His people. The covenantal lifestyle certainly is a secret even within the church, much less the broader society. But the Lord is doing just as He promised and is showing His covenant to those who fear Him. To use a Biblical term, the faithful have often been a remnant through history and there is that feeling again now in America. The church is large but it is also largely unfaithful in some of the most important things, education being one of the foremost. Homeschooling is a mark of the remnant in our time.

Being in the minority can be disconcerting that is for sure. When our forefathers left England and Holland for America they also were a minority. It is interesting to read that it was largely due to a concern for the spiritual welfare of their children that they made the journey. Writing about the Pilgrim's plans to leave Holland William Bradford states,

> But that which was more lamentable, and of all sorrows most heavy to be borne, was that many of their children, by these occasions and the great licentiousness of youth in that country, and the manifold temptations of the place, were drawn away by evil examples into extravagant and dangerous courses.[1]

88

For the sake of their children they decided to move to a dangerous new continent, risking everything in order to protect their children from the licentious culture in Holland. These few who were scorned for their radical obedience to Christ are still remembered for the greatness of their works and the success of their enterprise even though it was launched under small and humble means.

The Lord we serve is a jealous God who has always demanded exclusive worship. The words He spoke to his covenant people under Moses are still relevant today:

> Take heed to thyself, lest thou make a covenant with the inhabitants of the land whither thou goest, lest it be a snare in the midst of thee: But ye shall destroy their altars, break their images, and cut down their groves: For thou shalt worship no other god: for the Lord, whose name is Jealous, is a jealous God: Lest thou make a covenant with the inhabitants of the land, and thou go a whoring after their gods, and do sacrifice unto their gods, and one call thee, and thou eat of his sacrifice; And thou take of their daughters unto thy sons, and their daughters go a whoring after their gods, and make thy sons go a whoring after their gods.

**Exodus 34:12–16**

We have forgotten that the Lord is a jealous God. Many church members have effectively made covenants with the unregenerate in the land. They have little concern for maintaining a life separate from that of what has become an alien culture. Churchmen want to be at perfect peace with a culture that regards Biblical faith as an embarrassment. They "do sacrifice unto their gods" by offering their children as sacrificial lambs in the classrooms of the enemies of Christian faith. The result of this covenantal unfaithfulness on the part of Christian families is that their children do exactly as discussed in the Exodus passage. Their sons and daughters marry outside the faith, thus cutting off the Godly covenant progression within their families. The Christian family is transformed into a family where the sons and daughters "go a whoring after other gods."

For some reason many Christians are against the concept of living lives separate from the culture. They seem to believe that by immersing their families, including children, fully into the society they will avoid becoming too narrow. They also hope to win some of the surrounding lost by the influence of their Godly children. The Scripture from Exodus thirty-four gives a completely different view. It teaches us to value separateness for its ability to protect our families, keeping them in the proper covenant relationship with their Creator. A separate life is to be pursued not scorned. As to its being too narrow, let that be judged by the One who calls Himself a jealous God. Narrowness is implicit for our relationship with Him to succeed.

## THE TENOR OF THE WORDS

At the conclusion of this passage in Exodus God instructs Moses saying, "…write thou these words: for after the tenor of these words I have made a covenant with thee and with Israel" (Exodus 34:27). The tenor of His words is that to which we need to be giving our attention. The passage (Exodus 34:8–27) is too long to detail here but it is filled with specific instructions as to how God is to be served and obeyed. It marks out behavior that sets Israel apart from the surrounding nations. The nation was to be marked by its living separate unto the Lord. We do not live by the laws of the offerings and sacrifices any longer. Those parts of the law were fulfilled in Christ. However, it is still true that His covenant with us is after the tenor of those words. The tenor is that of a separate people who choose to obey their God rather than being at peace with the surrounding culture. The way we educate our children is to be in response to the tenor of those words. It is the tenor of the covenant.

Those who live in covenant with Christ have this promise:

Now therefore, if ye will obey my voice indeed, and keep my covenant, then ye shall be a peculiar treasure unto me above all people: for all the earth is mine.

**Exodus 19:5**

We have set before us a choice: will we join the culture and find our treasure there or do we value the ways of God above that of men? Jesus told us that where our hearts are there will our treasure be also. The condition of the heart is crucial here. Are our hearts longing to please God or to please man? Will we be God's peculiar treasure through the keeping of His covenant? Home education is necessary to advance covenant faithfulness.

# Chapter 7

# Additional Considerations

---

For the time will come when they will
not endure sound doctrine; but after their
own lusts shall they heap to themselves
teachers…

**2 Timothy 4:3**

## Possible Mistakes

Often the objections against home education have to do with possible mistakes that may be made by the homeschooling family. These include a variety of possible errors. In fact the mistakes being warned against sometimes include supposed problems that are exact *opposites* in the behavior of the child. For instance I have on my desk a book on education that contains a section about *shyness and over confidence* where the author views homeschool parents as producing children who often fall into these behaviors. He thinks of shyness and overconfidence as particularly springing from the homeschooling environment.

This of course is just hoo-hah. Does anyone believe that schools produce all perfectly balanced children who display the exact Biblically mandated portions of both shyness and confidence? In fact how would anyone define what that perfect balance is? In his mind any deviation from some undefined ideal standard of interactive behavior is an indication that the homeschooling has been defective. Is the child shy? It was that oppressive homeschool environment. Is the child not very shy? It was that permissive homeschooling that lets the kids back talk everybody. This kind of analysis is insufferable. It condemns home education no matter what the outcome and presumes that schools produce the ideal Christian personality. They do not.

A second supposed error often warned against is that the children will not receive a real education; the parents may not have enough discipline to teach and the children will just mess around the house never studying what they ought. These kinds of accusations are based on the rare exceptions not the norm. Numerous studies have already proven that home educated students far out-perform their peers in academics. So there is really not much to argue about here. The nay-sayers will always be looking for something to carp about. It is not only the modern studies that give evidence for the excellence of the home education model. Our nation's founding fathers reported some of the best literacy rates in the world for their colonies during that era, when most students learned at home. Everyone knows there will be a tiny number of families that do a lousy job teaching their children but it will always be fewer than the number of students left behind in the schools. Besides all of this our theology ought to inform us that the Spirit of God is working in Christian families to empower them to do the right thing. Surely the Holy Spirit is sufficient to accomplish His work in our families. We do not need to bypass His labors by handing over the privilege of teaching to an institution, however well intentioned that school might be.

# MASS PRODUCED STUDENTS

Mass produced students are the product of mass education. The students are picked up in large numbers by the same orange bus every day. They all have to choose (if choice is allowed) from the same narrow listing of classes—many of which are of questionable value and a few that are either useless or contain immoral content. The students all learn from the same teachers, go to the same in-school doings, hear the same special speakers, and attend the same extra-curricular events. They crowd into the officially approved eating area, everybody has the same kind of locker, they all use the same textbooks and... well, you get the idea.

Schools are about mass production and conformity. This type of manufacturing works great for TV sets and toasters. It is a good idea out of place when applied to education. The Biblical model for teaching is **personalized tutoring by parents**. This is not something that can be exchanged for a factory model of teaching. There has been a lot of talk lately about classical Christian schools being the best answer to Christian educational needs. Unfortunately, however well planned the school may be, it will still deliver mass produced education in violation of Biblical principle. Classical education can be good but taking the students out of the home for most of the day, five days a week, to receive that instruction still violates Biblical teaching. Somewhere along the way Christian parents just need to decide that God is right and go with that.

Some reformed Christians are promoting the Christian school model as being an extension of the covenantal mandate. They view it as the community of God's people advancing together. This idea is purely a made up notion of the covenant—very emotional but not grounded in good doctrine. It misapplies the premise and basis of covenantal living. Obedience to God's law, a common faith, a church ordered after Biblical tenets, common worship, Biblical fellowship and feasts, and a church community that works to reproduce itself generationally will build a covenant community. We should not disobey God in the form of our education practices so that we can (supposedly) please Him with a new way to extend covenantal living. It is not covenantal living.

Mass education ignores issues of the heart and of the individual gifts with which God has blessed our children. The Apostle Paul told Timothy, "Neglect not the gift that is in thee…" (1 Timothy 4:14). A significant part of our work as parents is to teach our children such that their gifts are exercised by practice, making ready for future ministry. Schools with their mass education techniques cannot do this. The gifts are given first to individuals not first to covenant communities. Therefore they must be exercised and developed within individuals. Schools with their mass teaching approach tend to crush the spirit and hold back the development of spiritual gifts and skills. If we want to see another age of great Christian leaders we will likely have to do the things that produce them. This will include developing gifted people—training up our children in the way they should go. Schools are much too impersonal to accomplish this. By their nature schools produce a bland, leveling sameness, chopping off the heads so to speak, of the most exemplary students. Most are inculcated with the spirit of mediocrity, inoculating them against true greatness. To blend into the crowd is to succeed. This is what schools do best. They produce students that are like everyone else. The most highly rewarded attendees are the ones that best match the school's paradigm for approved social character. Real greatness rarely springs from such infertile soil. America's children need to be returned to their homes. It is God's plan and it is the garden that grows the most magnificent fruit.

## BUILDING FAMILY UNITY

Part of the discussion that needs to take place concerning how we do schooling has to do with how our education decisions affect the family and its unity. If the family really is the basic building block of society (and it is), then we need to think about how education works within the family to further God's purposes for it. Christians in our time accept school as being a given and then fit the family needs around whatever demands the schools make. Does the school require the student to be there every week day for nine months? Well, OK, we just send them. Does the school demand that the student do homework several evenings a week? Once again we structure the family schedule to accommodate that demand. Are there special programs, sporting contests, parent teacher meetings, a cookie sale to help pay the national debt (that really happened), prom, detention or any other number of events? The parents are expected to make sure their child is not left behind. Being left behind by the schools is about like being left behind by the Titanic. At first you feel like you missed something but later on you brag to your friends about how smart you were for not being there. It is always discomfiting to go against the crowd at the start. One of the big problems with the schools is that they dominate the schedules for our families. It is OK to slight the needs of the family but do not miss anything at school or you are a bad student (or parent) is how the logic works. Nobody says it this bluntly but the message is communicated in a thousand ways every day. Try missing class to go on a family outing for a couple of months and see what happens.

Family unity is the result of a family building lives together. They have to do work together, and talk, and pray for each other. There needs to be a sense of toiling as a group to build God's kingdom. They are mutually moving ahead with the duties the Lord has given their family. The fact that God covenants with families through the generations gives us good cause to believe that His desire is for families to work together for the furtherance of His work in this world. This being the case it is reasonable to talk of the family ministry or mission. Our family mission is Mission to Restore America. We have formalized the name and have worked to make it effective.

Every family need not copy what we have done but families ought to be unified in important activities and ministry. By working together we develop bonds that last a lifetime. We also create a family identity. The family identity gives a structure that anchors us in home and relationships having real history and substance. We are not just individuals occupying the same space. There is purpose in all we do. We are kingdom builders that God has assembled to encourage one another and accomplish worthy goals. Our tasks are not lonely projects. They are done in unity and joy.

Home education is a part of a properly functioning family. It is not an outside activity. It is a central activity that leads to greater goals. It is also a part of a healthy family practice of reading and studying to show ourselves approved before God. Study is a Christian virtue. One of the best ways to unify a family is to discuss Scripture and good books together. Common ideas and experiences bond people for life. Schools work against this bonding by giving the students a life outside the family. When the children are older and ready to leave home then they need to have more separate lives. But when they are in childhood they need to work in unity with their family. This gives moral and emotional stability that will make them excellent parents in the future. School is not an extension of the family and the family is not an extension of the school. Rather, school is an historical aberration that is robbing families of the unity God desires.

## SALT AND LIGHT

One of the most popular reasons Christian parents give for keeping their children in the government schools is that they want their children to be salt and light. The parents understand that the schools are corrupt and that the teaching will not be based in Biblical thought. But in their minds the importance of reaching the lost out-weighs any other consideration. The child is viewed as a missionary. Of course he has not been trained as a missionary. Real missionaries spend long periods of study learning to understand the culture into which they are being sent. They also master the Scriptures and theology so they can have some good idea as to how to reach the people without compromising their own faith.

Child missionaries have none of these advantages. They have not even learned Biblical doctrine much less how to convert others to it. The whole idea that we should send children to evangelize the teachers is silly beyond words. The theory that five year olds are going to go head to head with their thirty year old teachers and convert them is a most unlikely scenario. The fact is that the majority of parents would consider that to be a thankless task. Yet somehow Johnny and Suzie are supposed to be sent in to do the impossible. Evangelism does not work this way. I can find no Scripture to show that our children are to be the shock troops for evangelizing anyone, including school teachers or other students. This whole idea is theologically flawed. God never intended it to be the object of child education. We have other things we are supposed to be doing with our kids.

The concept of Christian children evangelizing the schools brings to mind the children's Crusade. Adult soldiers had failed to obtain all of their objectives in earlier crusades. Eventually European parents allowed the children to try marching to the Holy Land. The children's crusade ended in total disaster. The ones that did not die of hardships were made slaves along the way. They never made it to the battlefield and never conquered any enemies. They would have been much better off to have stayed home and received proper training if they were going to fight in those wars. The same is true of Christian children today. They need to be prepared for battle before being sent off to war. David did beat Goliath but it was not a normal event.

Christian children that are sent into the enemy education camp usually become slaves of the opposition. Besides all of the humanist influences, outright lies, and moral and multicultural rubbish being thrown at them, the students also have to deal with the adverse effects of being in proximity with Godless peers. Every day their faith will be discouraged and sometimes mocked outright. The Christian students cannot write a paper or make a speech that is distinctively Christian. Students are being told they cannot pray out loud over their lunch or with their friends. The Apostle Paul taught that "Bad company corrupts good morals" (1 Corinthians 15:33). Schools are the best places in our culture to apply this doctrine. There could not be a more accurate application. If Paul's words do not apply there they do not apply at all. Your child's morals will be corrupted if he attends school due to the many students there that make bad company. The direction is inevitable. It is another one of those places where we just need to agree that God is right.

We discovered the truth of this with our first daughter. As a young girl she was the sweetest little person. She was kind and forgiving and joyful almost all the time. We kept her home for kindergarten and taught her some ABCs. When it was time for first grade we decided to place her in a local Christian school. The school was connected to our church. It employed fine Christian teachers with the best of intentions. The problem is that the school experience transformed our daughter into a very different person. She became a difficult child. She began to treat her siblings just like she was treated at school by her peers. Her classmates were not delinquents. However, they also were not mature Christians. The other students acted like, well, six year olds. This was not a good group from which to learn her social skills. We wanted her to be a maturing Christian in all her behavior. The school environment turned around the progress that had been made at home. After seeing the effect of a good school on a good child we decided to bring her home. It was one of the best decisions we ever made. Like many other Christian parents we knew what the Scriptures said about parents teaching their children but we did not accept that doctrine fully at face value. We were captured for that one year by the spirit of the age that says our children must be in school or they will be wrecked. Now we know better and encourage others not to be captured by that same spirit.

# WE MUST PREPARE THEM FOR THE REAL WORLD

Another one of the arguments against home education is that children have to be prepared to live in the real world. I believe the perception is that the child that grows up at home is like a prisoner who after a lengthy sentence does not know how to make it on the outside. This is really an amazingly cynical view of the family and home.

There are a lot of assumptions that lie behind that point of view, one of the chief of which is that school prepares children for real life. No one contests that real life, (in other words adult life), as a general rule, begins after school is finished. So by definition real life as they call it is the years after you leave the institutions and learn to make it on your own. Consequently everybody agrees that life lived in an institution is not real life. This being the case I have to ask, "Then why do so many parents believe that spending thirteen years in an institution is the best preparation for life on the outside?" And to follow up, "Why do so many parents believe that life on the outside is bad preparation for life on the outside?" It is manifestly obvious that life in an institution is nothing like life in the real world, which is the point of forcing people to remain in them. Public prisons and schools, both being compulsory, do not prepare their occupants well for private life.

In real life young men and women are physically ready to be married and start families in their late teens. If they are Christians they view the Biblical injunctions against lust and fornication with great seriousness. It is better to marry than to burn, as the Apostle directs. Yet at age eighteen the typical schooled individual is far from ready for marriage and family. He is not ready to start a career and is psychologically a child. His preparedness for real life is woefully inadequate although his hormones do not agree. The present system guarantees that society will be filled with adolescents in adult bodies. It is a sociological and moral disaster that will not end until we restructure education and family patterns to correspond with the real world. Young men and women should be educationally and psychologically ready for adult life by their late teens. The created order in biology reflects the perfect mind of God. The reason that men and women are not ready for marriage at an early age has everything to do with the failure of the present organization of things to address these issues correctly. God got it right but we have not.

One of the inherent problems with school is that it creates this extended adolescence. The way the system works is that at age eighteen a young man finishes high school and ought to be ready for adult life, but he is not. In fact in almost every case he has no job skills and his education is so lacking that he must attend a trade school or college just to have some good hope of being able to start a successful career. At the end of his schooling he still has no adult career experience. His adult life has not yet begun and he is in his mid-twenties or often approaching thirty years old. His psychological maturity is hardly beyond what it was as a teenager. Therefore he does not feel ready to marry for several more years.

Young Christian women find themselves in a similar dilemma. Even if they have a Biblical view of family and marriage they still are faced with the fact that there are almost no men their age ready for adult responsibilities. Consequently the young ladies find themselves in need of career skills so they can support themselves for what may be a decade before a qualified Christian man struggles his way through the system and finally grows up.

Attending school does not prepare people for adult life but rather delays maturity. Home education, when done correctly, gives families the chance to rear children that are ready to join the real world of work and service much younger. As a home schooling parent I was able to bring my son with me to work from an early age. I remodeled buildings for a living and he started helping me before his tenth birthday. At first he fetched tools for me and picked up. As the years passed I taught him how to use the tools, do layout work, and run a crew. Working one day a week through his high school years he became a competent carpenter. Since the operation was home based he also learned quite a bit about running a small business. In fact I made it a point to teach him as much as possible about every aspect of it. At age twenty-one he acted as my carpentry crew foreman on a large commercial project, telling forty year old men what to do. By age twenty-two he was married, had started his own business, and was shopping for baby clothes. That is real life and he was prepared for it. He got a good education but he was also emotionally mature and sufficiently skilled to advance in the adult world. I know from practice that the extended immaturity fostered by the schools is not necessary, nor is it preferable from a Biblical perspective.

## THE FAILURE OF PUBLIC EDUCATION

Other authors have written much on the dangers and destruction connected with public education. Therefore I have limited my comments.

It is easy for parents to assume that their children are receiving a good education in the government schools. Typically they view their own education as having been adequate and so assume that their children are receiving a similar experience. Having studied virtually no history as relates to education the parents lack a ruler by which to judge the product being received. The decline of the system is slow enough that it is not detected through casual observation.

However, anyone that studies education knows that present standards are the lowest they have ever been in this nation. Here are a few bits of evidence I have discovered for my assertion that instruction used to be much better in the past.

- Our forefathers recorded that literacy rates in the colonies were above 95%

- One very popular textbook for high school age students was the brilliant Reformation era *Vindicia Contra Tyrannos,* (the case against tyrants)—typically read in Latin. Most students today would hardly be able to grasp it in English due to the need to follow extended logical arguments and careful Bible interpretation. Modern students do not have the practiced mental discipline required.

- The entrance requirements for all colleges in early America (up until well into the 1800s in many cases) demanded that the prospective student be able to translate documents (usually parts of the Bible) from Latin into Greek and vice-versa. A mastery of English was just an assumed condition. These requirements disappeared after Public Education became the norm.

- The best seller *Lex Rex* contains extensive quotes in Latin, some Greek, and a bit of Hebrew. It would not have been so well received by the masses if they could not understand it. Yet this book greatly informed the thinking of our ancestors.

- The typical vocabulary of an American two hundred years ago was 25,000 words. The normal vocabulary of modern schooled students now stands at 10,000 words.

- This is doubly important because we think using words. A lack of words reduces the ability to think with precision. It dumbs down the population making the inability to think accurately axiomatic.

- Cashier clerks used to be able to count change.

- The beauty of expression found in books written prior to the advent of government education is often striking. Many of those old histories etc. will make you weep for the beauty of the language. Modern books do not do that.

Here is an interesting observation about the state of American education by Paul Fussel from his book *Class*:

> The middle class is predominantly the audience for the numerous "new translations" (*rewritings* would be a better term) of the Bible which stigmatize our age. It's notable that these new versions were not thought necessary until universal education was said to have become widespread. So unfortunately educated as to be puzzled by any form of

English but the contemporary, with no sense of the history not just of ideas but of styles and idiom, the middle class requires that even its divinity be couched in "language that is easy to understand." ...the middle class hates and fears language, and in effect it insists that a class separation take place between those who relish

*Whither thou goest I will go (Ruth, 1:16)*

And the version they like,

*Where you go, I will go*[1]

So it is that we find ourselves at the beginning of the twenty-first century claiming to be the most enlightened people on earth but unable to appreciate anything pertaining to class or beauty. We assume our own comeliness having become coarse unaware.

Nothing will save government education. Designed as a godless attack on high Christian culture its nature is to bring low Christendom at every point. Thus it reduces both itself and all it touches. Those who believe that the professional educationists can rise again, flagellate each other with the words physician heal thyself, assuming that more strenuous attention to detail will revitalize the dying mass. Government education has become terminal but it will be a while before the carcass is abandoned.

## WHAT ABOUT COLLEGE?

For many families there is an assumption that their children must all attend college. It is often not even questioned. It should be. Now, I am not against all students receiving a college education. All of our children have at least two or more years behind them. The problems with seeking a college degree are many but there still can be good reasons for certain students to go anyway. For those that have identified a career path that requires a college degree it can be an excellent choice. A high percentage of college students do not fit this profile.

As many parents know, the college years are often little more than the extension of adolescence discussed above. The students often have no particular reason for being there except that someone told them it was important. This is evidenced by the vast number of students who cannot name their major even after a couple of years at the school. They are spending large sums of money for an education that has no real point except to keep them off the streets. The parents are hoping their child will find himself, but he is not even looking. By the time the post high school years arrive many students are so inoculated against real life that they can hardly imagine what else to do except to go to college. Since most of the colleges being attended are low class institutions they confer no heightened ability to earn income.[2] Parents ought to be rethinking the public school insistence that getting a job is the *Summum Bonum* of educational purpose. It is proletariat in its root resisting a more Biblical ideal of building family capital and a business. Schools can be good at producing future employees. They have no ability to train up entrepreneurs, originality and daring not being the skills rewarded in institutions generally. Schooled Christian young people will make good employees for their better educated, homeschooled peers. This however, is no reason to keep churning out job-oriented graduates. Government schools will produce an adequate number of job seeking "human resources" as long as remedial reading and counting classes remain available.

The reason that children cannot figure out what to do with themselves after the high school years is that the church and family failed to instill in them Biblical precepts for life. They have been taught a narrow version of the Christian faith that speaks only of personal morality and evangelism. If the student knows he is not called to the pastorate or the mission field then there is nothing left to do that really matters; at least that is the message communicated by a thousand different means from the churches. The Biblical ideals of expanding the covenant people, taking dominion over the land as directed in Genesis, and building Biblical culture have never been taught to many evangelicals and so they see no point in pursuing

106

those courses. They are unexcited about starting a family and rearing children because they attach little value to them. Therefore college is the acceptable option at hand. It keeps young people busy and delays entry into adulthood.

One of the sad things about attending college for many students is that they still do not know what they want to do even after graduating. This is because college does not give direction. God has already given general principles and therefore general direction for His people through His word. Having abandoned Godly principles Christians seek answers somewhere else. Shiny young faces arrive each fall at the university doors waiting for the institution to give them what they should have gotten at home. It is a hopeless task. Parents can minister to individuals and help them discover their gifts and Godly track for life. It is much more difficult for a school to do this and we may be overly gracious to assume the schools are trying. Attending college is not a good means to fix what was left undone in the home.

## THE FUTURE OF HOMESCHOOLING

There are several reasons to have high hopes for the future of homeschooling in America. One of them is the continuing decline in the government schools. During the past few decades academics have descended faster than a bobsled at the Olympics. Still, the teachers and those who speak and write for the public school monopoly refuse to acknowledge the need for revamping the system in any meaningful way. Their intransigence will continue to push people toward alternative ideas.

Meanwhile the growth in home education has continued unabated at a rate of about 15% per year for over a decade. I cannot prove it but I believe that this rate of growth probably reflects the rate at which the homeschool community is able to train and assimilate its disciples. Homeschoolers teach each other how to get started and what to do to progress. They often form small co-ops for one day a week fellowship. All of this takes time and energy, although gladly given in almost every case.

The good news for homeschool proponents is that due to the disdain in which they are held by the government school elitists, home educators tend to be overlooked by them. This is not universal but when the enemy is out of sight it is natural that they be forgotten. During the 1980s when laws were being challenged and homeschooling was new there were many important victories for the little people who just wanted to be left alone to teach their children. There has been a level of continued resistance to homeschooling by the hard core public educationists but not enough to slow the movement.

Eventually the legal battles against home school families will resume in greater force than ever. Growth in home education has always been fast but the numbers were small enough that it did not seriously threaten government ownership of education in America. Now things are changing. At a growth rate of 15%, homeschoolers double every five years. Five percent of all students in the country (two million + out of a total of forty-seven million) are now taught at home. In just five years that number should swell to 10% and in ten years to 20% if present trends continue; and they likely will continue. Homeschooling is now going second generation. The young people that are a product of home education are almost all determined to continue the tradition. Very few of these people will even consider the possibility of placing their children in a school. Plus, they have the advantage of having the confidence of experience and grandparents eager to assist in the work. Schools are irrelevant to these families.

The importance of the rate of growth is likely to remain unnoticed for a while yet by the defenders of government education. They are still in a partial state of denial as to the actual numbers. Researchers on the inside of the homeschool culture are estimating two million students taught at home (recent numbers from HSLDA).

The enemies of this Christian practice regularly report many fewer as evidenced by an article by CBS News released October 14, 2003 titled *Home Schooling Nightmares,* which states, "It is estimated that 850,000 children in this country are home-schooled." As often happens, the humanist influencers of culture believe their own lies. In this case being underestimated should work to the advantage of the Christians who want to quietly raise up Godly seed. Why bother them if their numbers are small?

The math does tell us that there is an earthquake coming. The numbers are now sufficiently large that a doubling every five years shifts massive numbers away from the government schools. We are no longer counting in thousands we are calculating in millions. Forty years ago when black voters made up about ten percent of the population they were able to create a voting block sufficiently strong that they garnered great attention from the political parties, particularly the Democrats. In another ten years homeschoolers will have achieved that same percent of the vote and will become politically dangerous to those who wish to oppress them. The always inflexible teacher's unions, teacher's schools, local tax authorities, and the Democratic party will all have common cause to shut down the home schools and force compliance with their government owned cabal. A significant percentage of homeschool parents will go to jail to defend their rights believing it is wicked to place their children in the schools, especially the government schools. Philosophical lines will be drawn and battles will ensue.

## A FEW WORDS ABOUT COURAGE

Parents and the church are now confronted with difficult choices concerning how we will teach and rear our children. The culture around us rages against all things Christian. It is a formidable task to figure out what to do, much less do it. Parents have few examples by which to find inspiration for the wise and separate lives to which we have been called. Educational practices that would have been viewed as absurd throughout most of history have been made normal by the culture. Our society generally views anyone that violates its norms as kind of crazy or even dangerous. The day after 9/11, the twin towers having gone down, one of my close relatives asked me, "Have you been taking any flying lessons lately?" These kinds of insults will be thrown at anyone who follows the Good Shepherd. As Isaiah proclaims, "He was despised and rejected of men." His disciples will receive similar treatment if obedient to His word. If the world finds nothing about us to reject we have probably not displayed any courage in our pursuit of the kingdom. The faithful church and the world are going to be at war. It is what we should expect, but take courage for He has overcome the world.

## Chapter 8

# How Do I Get Started?

## Homeschool Organizations Nationwide

This list is current as of April 2006, but not exhaustive, and is intended to give you a place to start. There are many helpful organizations not listed here. Some of the best resources will come from recommendations by fellow homeschoolers in your area.

### Alaska

Alaska Private & Home Educators Association

Web    www.aphea.org
Phone  907-272-2998

### Alabama

Christian Home Education Fellowship of Alabama, Inc.

Web    www.chefofalabama.org
Phone  334-288-7229

## ARKANSAS

The Education Alliance

    Web    www.familycouncil.org
    Phone  501-375-7000

## ARIZONA

Arizona Families for Home Education

    Web    www.afhe.org
    Phone  602-235-2673

## CALIFORNIA

Christian Home Educators Association of California

    Web    www.cheaofca.org
    Phone  800-564-2432

## COLORADO

Christian Home Educators of Colorado

    Web    www.chec.org
    Phone  877-842-2432

Concerned Parents of Colorado

    Web    www.cpco.info
    Phone  719-748-8360

## CONNECTICUT

The Education Association of Christian Homeschoolers

    Web    www.teachct.org
    Phone  860-793-9968

## DISTRICT OF COLUMBIA

Christian Home Educators of DC

    Web    No Site
    Phone  202-829-5041

## DELAWARE

Delaware Home Education Association

> Web     www.dheaonline.org
> Phone    No Phone Number

## FLORIDA

Florida Parent-Educators Association, Inc.

> Web     www.fpea.com
> Phone    877-275-3732

## GEORGIA

Georgia Home Education Association

> Web     www.ghea.org
> Phone    770-461-3657

North Georgia Home Education Association

> Web     No Site
> Phone    706-861-1795

## HAWAII

Christian Homeschoolers of Hawaii

> Web     www.christianhomeschoolersofhawaii.org
> Phone    808-689-6398

## IOWA

Network of Iowa Christian Home Educators

> Web     www.the-NICHE.org
> Phone    515-830-1614

## IDAHO

Christian Homeschoolers of Idaho State

> Web     www.chois.org
> Phone    208-424-6685

## ILLINOIS

Christian Home Educators Coalition of Illinois

    Web    www.chec.cc
    Phone   773-278-0673

Illinois Christian Home Educators

    Web    www.iche.org
    Phone   847-603-1259

## INDIANA

Indiana Association of Home Educators

    Web    www.inhomeeducators.org
    Phone   317-859-1202

## KANSAS

Christian Home Educators Confederation of Kansas

    Web    kansashomeschool.org
    Phone   785-272-6655

## KENTUCKY

Christian Home Educators of Kentucky

    Web    www.chek.org
    Phone   270-358-9270

## LOUISIANA

Christian Home Educators Fellowship of Louisiana

    Web    www.chefofla.org
    Phone   888-876-2433

## MASSACHUSETTS

Massachusetts Homeschool Organization of Parent Educators

    Web    www.masshope.org
    Phone   508-829-0973

## MARYLAND

Christian Home Educators Network

 Web www.chenmd.org
 Phone 410-247-4731

Maryland Association of Christian Home Educators

 Web www.machemd.org
 Phone 301-607-4284

## MAINE

Homeschoolers of Maine

 Web www.homeschoolersofmaine.org
 Phone 207-763-2880

## MICHIGAN

Information Network for Christian Homes

 Web www.inch.org
 Phone 616-874-5656

## MINNESOTA

Minnesota Association of Christian Home Educators

 Web www.mache.org
 Phone 763-717-9070

## MISSOURI

Missouri Association of Teaching Christian Homes

 Web www.match-inc.org
 Phone 815-550-8641

Families for Home Education

 Web www.fhe-mo.org
 Phone 816-767-9825

## MISSISSIPPI

Mississippi Home Educators Association

Web    www.mhea.net
Phone    662-494-1999

## MONTANA

Montana Coalition of Home Educators

Web    www.mtche.org
Phone    406-587-6163

## NORTH CAROLINA

North Carolinians for Home Education

Web    www.nche.com
Phone    919-790-1100

## NORTH DAKOTA

North Dakota Home School Association

Web    www.ndhsa.org
Phone    701-263-3727

## NEBRASKA

Nebraska Christian Home Educators Association

Web    www.nchea.org
Phone    402-423-4297

## NEW HAMPSHIRE

Christian Home Educators of New Hampshire

Web    www.chenh.org
Phone    603-878-5001

## NEW JERSEY

Education Network of Christian Homeschoolers of New Jersey

Web     www.enochnj.org
Phone   732-291-7800

## New Mexico

Christian Association of Parent Educators—New Mexico

Web     www.cape-nm.org
Phone   505-451-7453

## Nevada

The Nevada Homeschool Network

Web     www.nevadahomeschoolnetwork.com
Phone   888-842-2602

Northern Nevada Home Schools

Web     www.nnhs.org
Phone   702-852-6647

## New York

Loving Education at Home

Web     www.leah.org
Phone   315-637-4525

## Ohio

Christian Home Educators of Ohio

Web     www.cheohome.org
Phone   740-654-3331

## Oklahoma

Oklahoma Christian Home Educators Consociation

Web     www.ochec.com
Phone   405-810-0386

Christian Home Educators Fellowship of Oklahoma

Web     www.chefok.org
Phone   918-583-7323

## OREGON

Oregon Christian Home Education Association Network

Web     www.oceannetwork.org
Phone   503-288-1285

## PENNSYLVANIA

Christian Home School Association of Pennsylvania

Web     www.chaponline.com
Phone   717-838-0980

## RHODE ISLAND

Rhode Island Guild of Home Teachers

Web     www.rihomeschool.com
Phone   401-351-5991

## SOUTH CAROLINA

South Carolina Association of Independent Home Schoolers

Web     www.scaihs.org
Phone   803-454-0427

South Carolina Home Educators Association

Web     www.schomeeducatorsassociation.org
Phone   803-772-2330

## SOUTH DAKOTA

South Dakota Christian Home Educators

Web     www.sdche.org
Phone   605-348-2001

## TENNESSEE

Tennessee Home Education Association

Web     www.tnhea.org
Phone   858-623-7899

# TEXAS

Christian Home Education Association of Central Texas

    Web     www.cheact.org
    Phone  512-450-0070

Family Educators Alliance of South Texas

    Web     www.homeschoolfeast.com
    Phone  210-342-4674

Home School Texas

    Web     www.homeschooltexas.com
    Phone  214-358-5723

Southeast Texas Home School Association

    Web     www.sethsa.org
    Phone  281-370-8787

North Texas Home Educators Network

    Web     www.nthen.org
    Phone  214-495-9600

# UTAH

Utah Christian Homeschool Association

    Web     www.utch.org
    Phone  801-296-7198

# VIRGINIA

Home Educators Association of Virginia

    Web     www.heav.org
    Phone  804-278-9200

# VERMONT

Christian Home Educators of Vermont

    Web     www.homeschoolvt.org
    Phone  802-365-4052

## WASHINGTON

Washington Association of Teaching Christian Homes

Web     www.watchhome.org
Phone   206-729-4804

Washington Homeschool Organization

Web     www.washhomeschool.org
Phone   425-251-0439

## WISCONSIN

Wisconsin Christian Home Educators Association

Web     www.wisconsinchea.com
Phone   262-637-5127

## WEST VIRGINIA

Christian Home Educators of West Virginia

Web     www.chewv.org
Phone   877-802-1773

## WYOMING

Homeschoolers of Wyoming

Web     www.homeschoolersofwy.org
Phone   307-322-3539

# INFORMATIONAL ORGANIZATIONS

### Alliance for the Separation of School and State

Web     www.sepschool.org
Phone   559-499-1776

Org. Type

A good source for finding out the history of education and the results of government involvement. Website contains articles, petitions, and news stories.

### Home School Legal Defense Association (HSLDA)

Web     www.hslda.org
Phone   540-338-5600

Org. Type

Non-profit advocacy organization established to defend and advance the constitutional right of parents to direct the education of their children and to protect family freedoms. Has information available on state and national laws governing homeschooling, links to Homeschool organizations, articles, pending legislation and court cases, statistical studies, etc.

### National Home Education Research Institute

Web     www.nheri.org
Phone   503-364-1490

Org. Type

Research, statistical data, facts, demographics, technical reports, etc. concerning homeschooling.


# CURRICULUM RESOURCES

### ABEbooks.com

Great for out-of-print books

### American Vision

Web     www.americanvision.org
Phone   800-628-9460

American History, Government, Law, Audio Seminars

### Calvary Reformed Presbyterian Church

Web    www.clearlight.com/~crpc/cwsc-old.html

Phone   757-826-5942

Audio tapes from the Christian Worldview Student Conference addressing many subject areas

### Cumberland Books

Web    www.cumberlandbooks.com

Phone   877-244-5184

Audio Cassettes/CD's discussing homeschooling and other useful topics

### Elijah Company

Web    www.elijahco.com

Phone   888-235-4524

### Foundation for American Christian Education (FACE)

Web    www.face.net

Phone   800-352-3223

Webster's 1828 Dictionary of the English Language is available from this company. It is the last dictionary to be written from an entirely Christian perspective.

### Lamplighter Books

Web    www.lamppostpublishing.org

Phone   800-326-9273

Variety of Curriculum

### Lifetime Books & Gifts

Web    www.lifetimebooksandgifts.com

Phone   863-676-6311

List of Homeschool conferences and book fairs, wide variety of books and curriculum, and out-of-print books

### The Mayflower Institute

Web    www.mayflowerinstitute.com

Phone  888-222-2001

American History, Foundations of Liberty

**Ross House Books**

Web  www.rosshousebooks.org

Phone  209-736-4365 ext 12

Theology, Philosophy, History, Law, Science, Culture

**Wallbuilders**

Web  www.wallbuilders.com

Phone  817-441-6044

Historical Documents, American History

**Veritas Press**

Web  www.veritaspress.com

Phone  800-922-5082

Classical Curriculum

**Vision Forum**

Web  www.visionforum.com

Phone  800-440-0022

# EXTRA-CURRICULAR ACTIVITIES & TUTORING ASSISTANCE FOR HOME SCHOOLED STUDENTS

**Nehemiah Institute**

Web  www.nehemiahinstitute.com

Phone  800-948-3101

PEERS® Christian Worldview Testing

**Patrick Henry College**

Web  www.phc.edu

Phone  540-338-1776

Distance Learning, Summer Camps

### Summit Ministries (Colorado)

Web    www.summit.org
Phone   719-685-9103
Conferences, Camps, Worldview Training

### TeenPact

Web    www.teenpact.com
Phone   888-343-1776
Equips and trains teens in leadership and involvement in politics, government, and public policy issues

### TeenWorks (Michigan)

Web    www.teenworks.net
Phone   517-627-9099
Seminars, Tutoring Assistance

### Tools 4 Life

Web    www.home.earthlink.net/~blaines-tools4life/index.html
Phone   706-340-5739
Training in Public Speaking

### Worldview Academy

Web    www.worldview.org
Phone   830-620-5203
Camps, Conferences, Worldview Leadership Training

# SPECIAL NEEDS HOMESCHOOLERS

### National Challenged Homeschoolers Associated Network

Web    www.nathhan.org
Phone   208-267-6246

# USEFUL SUBSCRIPTION PUBLICATIONS

### Homeschooling Today

Web     www.homeschooltoday.com

Phone   No Phone Number

This site has a list of Homeschool conferences and curriculum fairs nationwide, as well as the *Homeschooling Today* magazine.

### Wisdom's Gate

Web     www.homeschooldigest.com

Phone   No Phone Number

Home School Digest

### World Magazine

Web     www.worldmag.com

Phone   800-951-6397

Weekly news magazine reporting from a Christian perspective

# Referenced Works

## PREFACE

1 *Clergy in the Classroom.* Noebel, David; Baldwin, J. F.;
Bywater, Kevin. Summit Press: Manitou Springs CO. 1995.


## CHAPTER 1: TO IMPART A BIBLICAL WORLDVIEW

1 *Guinea Pig Kids 2002.* Video. Bachmann, Michele; Chapman,
Michael J. Maple River Education Coalition: St. Paul, MN.
2002.

2 *Academic American Encyclopedia.* Grolier Inc: Danbury, CT.
1973. pg 7.

3 Ibid pg 363.

4 Ibid pg 360.

5 *The Americans—The Democratic Experience.* Boorstin, Daniel
J. Random House: New York. 1973. pg 557.

6 *American Dictionary of the English Language.* Webster,
Noah.1828. Republished by Foundation for American Christian
Education: San Francisco, CA. 1995. Introduction, pg 25.

**7**  Ibid. pg 25.

**8**  *The Americans—The Democratic Experience*. pg 452.

**9**  *Himalayas*. Shirakawa, Yoshikazu. Abradale Press: Harry N. Abrams, Inc: New York. 1971. Introduction.

**10**  *Modern American Painting*. Boswell, Peyton Jr. Dodd, Mead & Co. 1939.

## Chapter 3: It is the Only Method God Allows

**1**  *Institutes of the Christian Religion*. Calvin, John. Trans. Beveridge, Henry. WM. B. Eerdmans: Grand Rapids, MI. 1989. pg 398.

## Chapter 4: To Socialize Our Children Properly

**1**  *Sociology*. Hess, Beth B.; Markson, Elizabeth W.; Stein, Peter J. Fifth Edition. Allyn & Bacon: Boston. 1996. pg 10.

**2**  *American Dictionary of the English Language*. Webster, Noah. 1828. Republished by Foundation for Amerian Christian Education: San Francisco. 1995.

**3**  *The American Heritage Dictionary*. Dell: New York. 1983. pg 649.

**4**  newswithviews.com. July 8, 2002.

**5**  *Clergy in the Classroom*. Noebel, David. Summit Press: Manitou Springs, CO. pg iv.

**6**  Ibid. pg 77.

**7**  *Humanist Manifestos I & II*. ed. Kurtz, Paul. Prometheus Books: Amherst, NY. 1973. pg 3.

# Chapter 5: Righteousness is the Goal

1   *Of Plymouth Plantation 1620–1647*. Bradford, William. The Modern Library: New York. 1981. pg 17.

2   *By This Standard*. Bahnson, Greg. Institute for Christian Economics: Tyler, TX. 1985. *The Institutes of Biblical Law*. Rushdoony, Rousas John. The Presbyterian and Reformed Publishing Co. 1973.

# Chapter 6: To Advance Covenant Faithfulness

1   *Of Plymouth Plantation 1620–1647*. Bradford, William. The Modern Library: New York. 1981. pg 25

# Chapter 7: Additional Considerations

1   *Class: A Guide Through the American Status System*. Fussell, Paul. Simon & Schuster: New York. 1983.

2   Ibid. pg 134.